YOUR PLACE ON GOD'S DREAM TEAM:
THE MAKING OF CHAMPIONS

BY
TONY COOKE

D1473640

Harrison House
Tulsa, OK

17 16 15 14   10 9 8 7 6 5 4 3 2 1

Your Place on God's Dream Team: The Making of Champions
ISBN: 978-160683-849-5
Copyright © 2014 by Tony Cooke

DEDICATION

This book is dedicated to Billy Coyne, a young man who was born with Down syndrome and loves Jesus with all of his heart. Billy is a vital part of the team at Harvest World Outreach Church in Greensboro, North Carolina, where his older brother Joe is the senior pastor. Billy serves as an usher and also counts the change from each offering. Wherever he goes, Billy takes flyers from the church and hands them out to everyone he meets; he is the church's number-one evangelist and PR person. Billy's dedication and joyful spirit inspire the rest of the church family, and he is rightly valued as an important part of the ministry.

CONTENTS

Tony Cooke has written another book that is just outstanding! This book will help anyone who is working with teams. *I love* Tony's sports examples, but, more than anything, I love the practicality of his teaching. It's so useful in everyday life and in working with our team. Thank you, Tony, for writing *Your Place on God's Dream Team: the Making of Champions.* We plan to use this book with our church team!

Mike Cameneti

Lead Pastor, Faith Family Church, Canton, Ohio

One of the greatest leadership principles I've ever learned is the importance of building a great team, which in turn builds a great ministry. Tony Cooke's book *Your Place on God's Dream Team: The Making of Champions* gives a complete picture of what that team should look like and where your part is on that team. This book is a must-read for anyone who is serious about building an effective organization.

Dennis Rouse

Pastor, Victory Church, Norcross, Georgia

This is another great book by Tony Cooke. *Your Place on God's Dream Team: The Making of Champions* reminds us of our high calling and points us to our divine purpose. The reader will be encouraged to lay aside selfish desires and work with the Body of Christ to fulfill the assignment that Christ has given us. I consider this a must-read for everyone who desires eternal things.

Gary Hoffman

Pastor, Faith Fellowship, Rocky Mount, Virginia

Tony Cooke is a leader of leaders and a gift to the Body of Christ! In *Your Place on God's Dream Team: the Making of Champions*, Tony lays out a strategy to equip you to reach your full potential. This book is practical, powerful, and a great read for all who want to thrive, and it's full of biblical principles that have the ability to take you and your team to whole new levels of unity, growth, and fruitfulness for the Kingdom. There is a kind of team that the Lord takes notice of and commands a blessing on. Tony's book will position you and your team for championship levels!

Kevin Berry

Pastor, Mount Hope Church, Lansing, Michigan

Tony does a great job blending natural wisdom and spiritual truths to bring together a book that will help you find your place on God's team! The truth in this book will help you reach your full potential in life!

Mark Butler

Pastor, Harvest Bible Church, Stockton, California

Wow, Tony hit a home run with this book! It opened up my eyes—both as a Christian and as the lead coach of one of God's teams. The nine principles are life changing! I'm looking forward to having our leaders and volunteers read this book. Their lives will never be the same!

Joseph Cameneti Sr.

Pastor, Believers Church, Warren, Ohio

Teams are made up of individuals. Great teams are made up of individuals with great character and qualities. Jesus said, "Whoever desires to become great among you, let him be your servant." In *Your Place on God's Dream Team: The Making of Champions*, Tony Cooke does an excellent job unveiling the character and qualities that enable teams to achieve greatness. I'm looking forward to placing this book into the hands of every Dream Teamer at Relate Church.

Chuck Ford

Pastor, Relate Church, Byram, Mississippi

Scripture reveals the Body of Christ as a unity of members working together to accomplish God's purposes on Earth. Recruited by God Himself, each member has been divinely gifted and skillfully placed by God in a position in which God has graced him to function. In his book *Your Place on God's Dream Team: The Making of Champions*, Tony Cooke provides revelation and insights designed to help every team member develop the character traits of a champion and become a productive player on Team Jesus. Holy Ghost-inspired and masterfully written, Tony's book will stretch individuals and strengthen churches for championship performance effectiveness. I highly recommended it with great expectation and enthusiasm. Go team!

Bill Anzevino

Pastor, Christian Assembly, Industry, Pennsylvania

Tony Cooke has once again hit a home run. As a champion for the local church, he has written another book that will help believers and churches reach their full potential. *Your Place on God's Dream Team: The Making of Champions* reveals what it looks like to be part of a championship caliber team. I am confident that after reading this book you will have more purpose, passion, and vision for your life. The insightful principles in this book are ones that anyone can apply. If you are looking to take your effectiveness to another level, this is the book you've been looking for!

Norm Dubois

Pastor, East Coast Believers Church, Casselberry, Florida

I have always loved sports. Though I never achieved great acclaim in any of the sports that I enjoyed, the team parallels have shaped most of my ideas as a leader. I played individual sports—golf, track, and tennis, but the sports that I enjoyed the most were the ones that involved a team. I enjoyed the camaraderie and sense of belonging that came from the team dynamics. Tony has communicated a message through this book that I can identify with. The comparisons between team concepts and God's objective on the earth will resonate with readers who appreciate teamwork in any context. The characteristics taught in this book are vital to the making of a champion. Any successful team can relate to these principles and up their game. By my own experiences in team activity, I can see the vital nature of each of the principles that Tony has shared. These principles are gems of wisdom that can help to avoid pitfalls, keep our focus, and ultimately make us successful.

Dr. Pat Murray

Senior Founding Pastor, The Living Word Church, Vandalia, Ohio

We are all created by God to be champions, but no one has won a championship without help. Every true champion has received much help, instruction, support, and encouragement to attain his goals. It may look like the individual won the championship, but in reality it was a team of supportive, passionate players all doing their part that truly won the victory. The championship traits given in this book can take us all from just *running* the race to *winning* the race. It is a great honor to recommend this book, because I know it will be a great help and inspiration to you.

Darrell Huffman

Pastor, New Life Church, Huntington, West Virginia

Most people spend their entire lives trying to be part of a team. We all want to belong to something that is bigger than ourselves. Tony Cooke reveals a great truth to us – that God Himself is offering us a spot on the greatest team of all – His Dream Team. The key to discovering your purpose in life is to discover God's purpose for you. God's Dream Team will open your eyes to a world of opportunities that God has for you. If you are looking to find fulfillment and lasting purpose, this is the book for you!

Steve Smotherman

Pastor, Legacy Church, Albuquerque, New Mexico

In his book, Tony opens up the thought process of a champion. You will enjoy the tremendous way he communicates the mindset that made some of the greatest champions of all time. No matter what our role in the family, work, or church, we can help our team succeed by applying the dynamics of team mentality and collaboration to develop a championship mindset in every area of our lives.

Mark Bintliff

Pastor, New Creation Church, Glenwood Springs, Colorado

Your Place on God's Dream Team is another home run by Tony Cooke just as you would expect if you know Tony or have read any of his previous books. Once you start reading it, you won't want to put it down. I highly recommend this book for all pastors and ministry leaders who want to develop a Championship Team to impact the Kingdom of God. Also, every Christian who serves in leadership or in the helps ministry and desires to be an effective and vital part of a Championship Team should read this book. It will inspire and equip you to rise to a higher level in your ministry and serving.

Denny Beavers

Pastor, Living Word Church, Jonesboro, Arkansas

If you have ever been a part of a winning team, you know the satisfaction that comes when the team accomplishes its goal. In "Your Place on God's Dream Team: the Making of Champions," Tony describes the traits of champions and what it takes to build the kind of team that God can use to impact the world. I highly recommend this book as a powerful resource if it is your desire to build a strong family, church, or business that honors the Lord Jesus Christ.

Bobby Marks

Pastor, Cornerstone Church, Dothan, Alabama

Your Place On God's Dream Team is a perfect example of Tony's God-given ability to take a truth such as teamwork, expound on it, and, through his thoughtful writing, bring the Body of Christ in concert to accomplish God's chief objective: WORKING together TO WIN together A LOST GENERATION of people.

Alongside the fresh wind of God, Tony is right on time, uniting us to reach out into our communities and win them through teamwork. As a former student under Tony and a fellow minister for the past 25 years, I have known Tony's writings to influence a new generation of ministers to keep the course and stay solid in pure doctrine. I believe *Your Place On God's Dream Team* is a must for every minister and Christian's study library! If Jesus transformed the twelve into champions that *turned the world upside down*, I believe God can empower us to do the same using the truths set forth in this book. Great job, Tony!

Eddie Trayers

Pastor, Family Worship Center, Springfield, Virginia

INTRODUCTION

There's nothing more exhilarating to behold than a group of people who help, support, and complement one another in the fulfilling of a noble cause. King David affirmed such unity.

> *How wonderful and pleasant it is when brothers live together in harmony!*
>
> *For harmony is as precious as the anointing oil that was poured over Aaron's head, that ran down his beard and onto the border of his robe.*
>
> *Harmony is as refreshing as the dew from Mount Hermon that falls on the mountains of Zion. And there the LORD has pronounced his blessing, even life everlasting.*
>
> *Psalm 133:1-3, NLT*

This kind of unity usually isn't the starting place in most relationships. Teams have to really get to know each other, work through many issues, overcome various obstacles, and establish winning strategies in order to experience this caliber of cohesion.

Remember the Titans is a great movie that portrays the story of a high school football team struggling to unify after two schools (one comprised of African American students, and one comprised of white) merged. In the movie, the team goes for a week of pre-season training at Gettysburg College, and Coach Herman Boone (played by Denzel Washington) takes the team out to one of the battlefields. Boone shares with his bitterly divided team about the hatred and strife that caused so many Civil War deaths on that battlefield and then says, "...take a lesson from the dead. If we don't come together right now on this hallowed ground, we too will be destroyed, just like they were. I don't care if you like each other or not, but you will respect each other. And maybe...I don't know, maybe we'll learn to play this game like men."[1]

Early in the movie, it's obvious that the racially split team members are not moving toward collaboration or cohesion in the slightest. Two of the star players, Gary Bierteer, the best white player, and Julius Campbell, the best African American player, have an intense exchange during a face-to-face confrontation. Some understandably shy away from this type of confrontation, but we need to realize that the only thing worse than a dysfunctional team is a dysfunctional team that pretends everything is okay.

When it comes to denial, it's been said that you can't fix a problem you don't have. Often, it's only through open and honest discussions that Proverbs 27:17 can be fulfilled: "As iron sharpens iron, so a friend sharpens a friend" (*NLT*). For a team to become the best it can be, players cannot ignore glaring problems or fail to be accountable to one another. There is a reason why the Apostle Paul told us to speak the truth in love to one another (Ephesians 4:15).

An important lesson from *Remember the Titans* is that it doesn't matter where a team starts, but it does matter that team members move in the right direction, that they identify and remove hindrances, and that they move together toward the right goal.

[1]*Remember the Titans*. Dir. Boaz Yakin. Buena Vista Pictures Distribution, 2000. Film.

In the movie *Hoosiers*, a small-town underdog team—the Hickory Huskers—is preparing to take the court to play for the coveted Indiana state basketball championship. In the locker room, one of the players says, "Let's win this one for all the small schools that never had a chance to get here." Another team member says, "Let's win for coach who got us here."[2] They were dreaming big, but the dream came true! As I wrote this book, I was mindful of all the pastors—spiritual coaches—who dream of building a re-markable team of leaders and workers, those who will work together helping local churches come alive in all of their potential, vibrancy, and fullness.

When God wants to do something in the earth, He always starts with a leader. That leader has a God-given assignment, but he can't do it alone. Even the best leader knows that a team must be built to help bring about God's desires and plan. But that team must be made of people who have the right stuff. While God always *starts* His work with a leader, it appears that He always endeavors to *finish* His work through a team.

Our society adores teams that are comprised of super-stars and celebri-ties. Perhaps no other team has been so celebrated or captured the mind of American sports fans like the 1992 U.S. Olympic basketball team. Along with legends such as Larry Bird, Magic Johnson, and Michael Jordan, it was clear that every member of the "Dream Team" was an outstanding, world-class player in his own right. No opponent even came close to beating the Dream Team. Defeating opponents by an average of more than forty-three points per game, the Dream Team took its place in the annals of athletic history.

---

[2]*Hoosiers*. Dir. David Anspaugh. Orion Pictures, 1986. Film.

The members of the '92 Dream Team were all superstars. Yet the members of the Dream Team that Jesus assembled were all completely ordinary. They were common people with regular lives. They had not distinguished themselves as great philosophers, scholars, orators, or achievers. Scripture makes no attempt to glamorize these twelve men; instead, we see them in all of their raw humanity. As He was training them, Jesus noted that (on occasion) they were slow learners and spiritually dense; they lacked faith and understanding and had hard hearts; and they were fearful and full of unbelief.

The disciples ultimately became a great team through their association with Jesus and by the influence of the Holy Spirit, but they had to overcome problems common to all: inferiority, pride, jealousy, foot-in-mouth disease, doubts, fear, failure, and so forth. They even slept through some of their most crucial times of training! But Jesus—the Captain of our salvation— saw beyond their faults and recognized their potential. He didn't see them only as they were, but He also envisioned all that they could become.

Jesus looked beyond the clumsiness and impulsivity of Peter and saw an empowered preacher. Jesus saw more than the rambunctious turbulence of John; He also saw the "Apostle of Love." Jesus acknowledged the checkered past of the woman at the well, but He also saw a transformed testifier. And Jesus looked beyond the rage of Saul of Tarsus and saw a church builder and an epistle writer.

One of the main lessons from the lives of the original twelve disciples is that if God can use *them*, then He can use *us*. And God will use us to the degree to which we yield to Him, cooperate with Him, and work with one another. The Church is God's "Plan A." There is no Plan B.

The Apostle Paul was a man who loved, valued, and relied heavily upon his team. He also wanted to see teams of leaders and workers established in every church he started. But he understood the "raw materials" from which these teams would be built, and he addressed them accordingly.

> *Take a good look, friends, at who you were when you got called into this life. I don't see many of "the brightest and the best" among you, not many influential, not many from high-society families.*
>
> *Isn't it obvious that God deliberately chose men and women that the culture overlooks and exploits and abuses, chose these "nobodies" to expose the hollow pretensions of the "somebodies"?*
>
> *That makes it quite clear that none of you can get by with blowing your own horn before God.*
>
> *Everything that we have—right thinking and right living, a clean slate and a fresh start—comes from God by way of Jesus Christ.*
>
> *That's why we have the saying, "If you're going to blow a horn, blow a trumpet for God."*
>
> *1 Corinthians 1:26-31, MSG*

This passage is especially meaningful to those who feel that they're not talented enough, not brilliant enough, or not gifted enough. We may start out rough around the edges, but God wants to take our lives and transform us, empower us, and form us into teams of believers who will work mightily and effectively for His glory in the earth.

Individual performances are great, but Jesus wants to build a Dream Team out of us. Maybe you've never had the joy of being part of a team, or maybe the teams you've been a part of have seemed more like the Keystone Cops or the Three Stooges than a real Dream Team.

As you read this book, you will notice the emphasis on both the spiritual and natural benefits of teamwork. If you're on a church or ministry team, you will benefit from the teachings in this book. And if you are simply trying to establish better teamwork in your marriage and family or with your co-workers, you will also benefit.

Former U.S. Congressman J.C. Watts said, "I tell young men and women all the time that if they take everything they learned on the football field, the basketball court, the baseball diamond, and apply those principles to the business arena, or to being a mom or dad, or to being an elected official, they'll work because they're universal. These lessons include an understanding of delayed gratification, which is the result of a lot of hard work that causes a mental toughness and the perseverance, sacrifice, and commitment it takes to excel. Team sports teach you the concept of 'big team, little me.'"[3] The ideals that make sports teams great are the same concepts that will enable all kinds of teams to succeed.

Success for us can impact lives far beyond personal records or team trophies, because God continues to build a team that will fulfill His dreams in

---

[3]THE GAMES DO COUNT by BRIAN KILMEADE. Copyright © 2004 by Brian Kilmeade. Reprinted courtesy of HarperCollins Publishers.

the earth and make its mark in eternity. Wherever you are in your personal development and wherever your team is in its progress, we all have room to grow and improve. God gave us His best, and it is my prayer that as you and your team apply the principles in this book using the chapter study questions as guides for further reflection, we'll be able to give God our best as well.

CHAPTER ONE

The Greatest Team Ever

"The unity of the Godhead was unmarred by discord. Father,
Son, and Holy Spirit delight to honor one another. 'I and my
Father are one' (John 10:30), Jesus claimed, implying they
were one not only in essence, but also in attitude and pur-
pose. The Persons of the Trinity cooperated for our redemp-
tion in perfect harmony and reciprocity. The Father planned.
The Son made the plan possible of realization by yielding up
His life to death on the cross. The Spirit bent His fiery ener-
gies to the implementation of the plan. It was His apprecia-
tion of this harmony that inspired our Lord to pray for His
followers: 'That they may be one, as we are' (John 17:11)."[4]

- Oswald Sanders

If you want to watch sparks fly among avid sports fans, just ask the
question, "Which is the greatest sports team of all time?" Basketball fans
might argue for Bill Russell's Celtics, for Kareem's Lakers, or for Michael
Jordan's Bulls. Baseball fans might nominate the 1927 Yankees with Babe
Ruth and Lou Gehrig, or the 1902 Pittsburgh Pirates with Honus Wagner, or
the 1975 Cincinnati Reds with Johnny Bench, Joe Morgan, and Pete Rose.

---

[4]Oswald Sanders, *The Incomparable Christ*, (Chicago, Moody Publishers, Chicago.
1971), 10

Football enthusiasts (as with any sport) might pull for their own favorite team, but some would choose the '85 Bears or the '72 Dolphins. Others would pull for the '62 Packers led by Bart Starr. We discussed the 1992 U.S. Men's Olympic basketball team—the Dream Team—in the Introduction, but let's not forget about "the Miracle on Ice," the 1980 U.S. Men's Olympic ice hockey team. American fans of women's sports would perhaps cite the U.S. women's national soccer team that won the World Cup in 1999. International readers might vote for the Brazil National football (soccer) team that won the World Cup in 1970, or the New Zealand All Blacks who have often dominated rugby on the international stage.

While people could argue ad infinitum about which sports team of all time was the greatest, there is another Team whose proficiency, perfection, and performance places it indisputably in a class by itself: the Trinity.

Team Trinity

There are not three Gods; there is one God who exists eternally in three persons. Neither is there one Person who simply takes on three different roles from time to time. There is one God who is eternally existent in three persons—the Father, the Son, and the Holy Spirit; these three are co-equal and co-eternal. The members of the Trinity—as with the members of any team—fulfill different roles and responsibilities. They also exhibit unparalleled respect and love toward one another. The pattern of their workings seems to be better understood and explained in the following way:

- **The Father plans;** He is the architect and the source of divine activity.

- **The Son performs;** He executes and carries out the Father's plan.

- **The Holy Spirit perfects;** He follows up and brings into reality that which the Father ordained and that which the Son has carried out.

Insightful believers have long recognized these workings. Basil of Caesarea (330-379 A.D.) said, "Every divine action begins from the Father, proceeds through the Son, and is completed in the Holy Spirit." Later, Puritan clergyman Thomas Manton expressed a similar thought: "The beginning of our salvation is from God the Father, the dispensation is from the Son, and the application from the Holy Ghost." In more recent times, author J.I. Packer wrote, "It is also true that the reality of the Father, the Son, and the Holy Spirit working together as a team for the full salvation of sinners pervades the entire New Testament."[5] Packer also referred to "the cooperative activity of the Three in saving us—the Father planning, the Son procuring, and the Spirit applying redemption."[6]

We see the seamless, flawless working of the Trinity in the following examples in Scripture:

- **The Annunciation:** "The Holy Spirit will come upon you, and the power of the Highest will overshadow you; therefore, also, that Holy One who is to be born will be called the Son of God" (Luke 1:35, *NKJV*).

---

[5] J.I. Packer, *Affirming the Apostles' Creed*, Wheaton, Illinois, Crossway Books, 2008, Page 19.
[6] J.I. Packer, *Affirming the Apostles' Creed*, Wheaton, Illinois, Crossway Books, 2008, Page 35.

- **The Lord's Baptism:** "When He had been baptized, Jesus came up immediately from the water; and behold, the heavens were opened to Him, and He saw the Spirit of God descending like a dove and alighting upon Him. And suddenly a voice came from heaven, saying, 'This is My beloved Son, in whom I am well pleased'" (Matthew 3:16-17, *NKJV*).

- **Insight of John the Baptist:** "For He whom God has sent speaks the words of God, for God does not give the Spirit by measure. The Father loves the Son, and has given all things into His hand" (John 3:34-35, *NKJV*).

- **Jesus' Ministry:** "How God anointed Jesus of Nazareth with the Holy Spirit and with power, who went about doing good and healing all who were oppressed by the devil..." (Acts 10:38, *NKJV*).

- **Jesus' Prayer:** "And I will pray the Father, and He will give you another Helper, that He may abide with you forever—the Spirit of truth." (John 14:16-17, *NKJV*).

- **Redemption:** "But when the kindness and the love of God our Savior toward man appeared, not by works of righteousness which we have done, but according to His mercy He saved us, through the washing of regeneration and renewing of the Holy Spirit, whom He poured out on us abundantly through Jesus Christ our Savior." (Titus 3:4-6, *NKJV*).

- **The Initial Receiving of the Spirit:** "So Jesus said to them again, 'Peace to you! As the Father has sent Me, I also send you.' And when He had said this, He breathed on them, and said to them, 'Receive the Holy Spirit'" (John 20:21-22, *NKJV*).

- **The Great Commission:** "Go therefore and make disciples of all the nations, baptizing them in the name of the Father and of the Son and of the Holy Spirit." (Matthew 28:19, *NKJV*).

- **A Ministerial Charge:** "Take heed to yourselves and to all the flock, among which the Holy Spirit has made you overseers, to shepherd the church of God which He purchased with His own blood" (Acts 20:28, *NKJV*).

- **Access to God:** "Now all of us can come to the Father through the same Holy Spirit because of what Christ has done for us" (Ephesians 2:18, *NLT*).

- **Teaching on Church Unity:** "There is one body and one Spirit, just as you were called in one hope of your calling; one Lord, one faith, one baptism; one God and Father of all, who is above all, and through all, and in you all" (Ephesians 4:4-6, *NKJV*).

- **Cleansing:** "How much more shall the blood of Christ, who through the eternal Spirit offered Himself without spot to God, cleanse your conscience from dead works to serve the living God?" (Hebrews 9:14, *NKJV*).

- **Assurance:** "By this we know that we abide in Him, and He in us, because He has given us of His Spirit. And we have seen and testify that the Father has sent the Son as Savior of the world" (1 John 4:13-14, *NKJV*).

- **Paul's Apostolic Greeting:** "This letter is from Paul, a slave of Christ Jesus, chosen by God to be an apostle and sent out to preach his Good News....The Good News is about his Son...he was shown to be the Son of God when he was raised from the dead by the power of the Holy Spirit" (Romans 1:1, 3-4, *NLT*).

- **Peter's Apostolic Greeting:** "This letter is from Peter, an apostle of Jesus Christ. I am writing to God's chosen people...God the Father knew you and chose you long ago, and his Spirit has made you holy. As a result, you have obeyed him and have been cleansed by the blood of Jesus Christ" (1 Peter 1:1-2, *NLT*).

- **An Apostolic Benediction:** "The grace of the Lord Jesus Christ, and the love of God, and the communion of the Holy Spirit be with you all. Amen" (2 Corinthians 13:14, *NKJV*).

- **In Heaven:** The Book of Revelation refers to "the Lord God Almighty" who "sits on the throne" (4:8-9). We also see "a Lamb as though it had been slain" (5:6). This Lamb is called "the Lion of the tribe of Judah" and "the Root of David" (5:5). And "...before the throne... are the seven Spirits of God" or, as the *NLT* renders it, "the sevenfold Spirit of God" (4:5).

It is absolutely amazing and captivating how God the Father, God the Son, and God the Holy Spirit have worked together for our good and our benefit. Our welfare depends upon the harmonious, synchronized, and collaborative work of the Godhead.

Let's look more in depth at a couple of examples in Scripture of the

Trinity's amazing teamwork.

The Trinity in Redemption

"Redemption" is the term used to describe the wonderful work by which God reclaimed and purchased mankind back to Himself, removing the barrier of man's sin and enabling us to enter into covenant relationship with Him. Simply put, God the Father *planned* redemption—He is the Architect; it was His will that was being carried out. God the Son *performed* redemption—He is the One who died and rose for us. God the Holy Spirit *reveals* redemption—He is the One who makes it real to us and in us, perfecting God's work in our lives.

In Ephesians 1:4, 7, and 13, we discover that the Father chose us; the Son redeemed us; and the Holy Spirit sealed us. Each member of the Trinity fulfilled a specific role; there was no jealousy among them and no jockeying for position. They were seamless in their unity even though they each contributed differently to the fulfillment of the plan. Each Member performed individually, yet each Member was also entirely interdependent, perfectly synchronized, and powerfully synergistic.

The Trinity in Creation

We also see the working of the Trinity in creation. If you ask a believer who created the universe, he or she will typically answer, "God." But if you ask which member of the Trinity actually did the work, you may not receive as confident a response.

In reality, all three members of the Trinity were involved in creation.

However, in John 1:3,[7] Colossians 1:16,[8] and Hebrews 1:2 and 10,[9] we discover that Jesus was the actual agent of creation; He created everything.

In Genesis 1:1, we read that "God created," yet we know that God created by speaking, and that Jesus is the Word (John 1:1,14). Then we read in Genesis 1:2 that in the midst of the darkness and chaos, "the Spirit of God was hovering over the face of the waters." The *Amplified Version* of Genesis 1:2 says, "The Spirit of God was moving (hovering, brooding) over the face of the waters."

The process of creation, then, is consistent with the divine pattern:

- **God the Father** *planned* creation—He is the Architect who commissioned that which was to be done.

- **God the Son** *performed* creation—He made all things.

- **God the Holy Spirit** *revealed* creation—He followed up on and finessed the work.

Even when it came to creating man, the "team effort" of the Trinity is clearly seen. Genesis 1:26 says, "Then God said, 'Let Us make man in Our image, according to Our likeness'" (*NKJV*).

Again we see harmonious partnership, with each member of the Godhead contributing and producing. Every member of "Team Trinity" is fully

---

[7]"All things were made through Him, and without Him nothing was made that was made" (John 1:3, *NKJV*).

[8]"For by Him all things were created that are in heaven and that are on earth, visible and invisible, whether thrones or dominions or principalities or powers. All things were created through Him and for Him" (Colossians 1:16, *NKJV*).

[9]"...has in these last days spoken to us by His Son, whom He has appointed heir of all things, through whom also He made the worlds...You, LORD, in the beginning laid the foundation of the earth, and the heavens are the work of Your hands" (Hebrews 1:2,10, *NKJV*).

invested in the process and the goal. No one is a spectator or observer. Everyone has a role and function. There is no jealousy, strife, or discord. No member possesses a secret personal agenda. Their work is seamlessly interdependent upon each other. It truly is, as was the motto of the three Musketeers, "One for all, and all for One."

How Does the Trinity's Teamwork Apply to Us?

Not only have the Father, Son, and Holy Spirit demonstrated the greatest teamwork ever, but Jesus also expressed His great desire that *our* teamwork—the unity and partnership exhibited by the Church—be patterned after and reflect the teamwork displayed by the Trinity. Consider what Jesus prayed right before He went to the Garden of Gethsemane.

> *I do not pray for these alone, but also for those who will believe in Me through their word; that they all may be one, as You, Father, are in Me, and I in You; that they also may be one in Us, that the world may believe that You sent Me.*
>
> *And the glory which You gave Me I have given them, that they may be one just as We are one:*
>
> *I in them, and You in Me; that they may be made perfect in one, and that the world may know that You have sent Me, and have loved them as You have loved Me.*
>
> *John 17:20-23, NKJV*

Even a casual reading of this passage reveals that the unity of His followers was an amazingly high priority to the Lord Jesus. Notice that this prayer was a trans-generational prayer. Jesus prayed this for all who would ever believe in Him.

For the sake of better understanding, let's reread this passage using a synonym in place of the word "one" and substitute the words "unity," "team," and "teamwork."

"I pray...that they may have unity and be a team, as You, Father, are in Me, and I in You; that they may also be unified as a team in Us...that they may be a unified team just as we are a unified Team...that they may be made perfect in their unity and teamwork just as we are...."

The potential impact Jesus described of this oneness, unity, or teamwork is earth shattering. Jesus said it would result in the world believing and knowing that God had sent Him and knowing that the Father's love for them was the same as His love for Jesus. The Lord did not indicate it would be the great sermons of the preachers or the great music of the worship team that would convince the world but, rather, the overall unity and teamwork of the Body of Christ.

Our Standard of Teamwork

Jesus did not pray that we would have unity in some vague, abstract way. No, He prayed that we would have the same type of unity that He and the Father shared. Likewise, Jesus does not command us to love one another in a general way, but He specifically says, "as I have loved you" (John 13:34; 15:12). There is a standard of quality that Jesus prescribes, one that necessitates our cooperation with His ability and His Spirit working in our lives in order for it to happen. We will never accomplish these feats of unity and love in our own natural strength.

So how did Jesus define the unity He desires for us? John 17 gives us the answer.

...that they all may be one, as You, Father, are in Me, and I in You; that they also may be one in Us...

...that they may be one just as We are one...

John 17:21-22, NKJV

Jesus desires that our relationships in the Body of Christ reflect the same quality of unity and cooperation as He experienced with the Father.

Even though the Holy Spirit's name is not mentioned in these verses of Scripture, I am convinced that He is inextricably interwoven into the very fabric of verses and into all the interactions in which the Father and Son have engaged. It is only fitting that we should acknowledge the Spirit's presence in Jesus' prayer, regardless of His name not appearing. It is so very like Him to inspire Jesus' very words while not drawing attention to Himself.

Through Scripture, we are convinced that it is Jesus' heartfelt, earnest prayer that our teamwork reflect the teamwork of the Trinity.

Quotes Worth Remembering

"Have we not one God and one Christ and one Spirit of grace shed upon us?"

- Clement of Rome

"Our salvation... is free in the Father, sure in the Son, ours in the Spirit."

- Thomas Manton

"If there be one God subsisting in three persons, then let us give equal reverence to all the persons in the Trinity. There is not more or less in the Trinity; the Father is not more God than the Son and Holy Ghost. There is an order in the Godhead, but no degrees; one person has not a majority or super eminence above another, therefore we must give equal worship to all the persons."

- Thomas Watson

"In the divine economy of man's salvation, election is the special work of God the Father: atonement, mediation, and intercession, the special work of God the Son: and sanctification: the special work of God the Holy Ghost."

- J.C. Ryle

"Within the Holy Trinity we see that in principle the notion of subordination does not carry with it the notion of inferiority...Christ willingly submitted to the Father, without a word of protest. It is precisely that willingness that we are called to imitate in submitting ourselves to authority."

- R.C. Sproul

Questions for Reflection and Discussion

1. Describe in your own words how the Trinity functions together in teamwork.

2. How essential is the unified and harmonized working of the Trinity to our own salvation? What if there had been discord, or if one

member of the Trinity had not fulfilled His assignment?

3. In what ways could we as believers pattern our teamwork after the Trinity? To improve, are there things we are not doing that we need to begin doing? Are there things we are doing that we need to stop?

4. What would you envision happening if our teamwork actually became more like that of the Trinity? What results would we see?

5. Review the five Quotes Worth Remembering. Which of these quotes speaks the most to you, and how does it specifically impact you?

CHAPTER TWO

Biblical Perspectives on Teams and Athletes

"To make a ball club a champion, the effort has to start with the bat boy and move right up to the owner."[10]

- Brooks Robinson

Earth's first couple was designed to function as a team; they were to be "one flesh" (Genesis 2:24). Sadly, instead of partnering collaboratively, Adam and Eve quickly fell into disunity and disarray. Adam failed to lead, standing passively by while Eve was deceived and yielded to temptation. When challenged, Adam quickly blamed Eve (Genesis 3:12), even though he, too, had disobeyed.

Marred by sin and stained by the Fall, humanity nonetheless retains a capacity that can incline us toward partnership and working with others. Noah's descendants embraced the idea of teamwork. Genesis 11:1 tells us that "the whole earth had one language and one speech." Not only did the people share a common language, but they also embraced a common purpose.

And they said, "Come, let us build ourselves a city, and a tower whose top is in the heavens; let us make a name for

---

[10]Dr. Criswell Freeman, *The Wisdom of Old Time Baseball*, (Nashville, TN, Walnut Grove Press, 1996), Page 140.

ourselves, lest we be scattered abroad over the face of the whole earth."

But the Lord came down to see the city and the tower which the sons of men had built.

And the Lord said, "Indeed the people are one and they all have one language, and this is what they begin to do; now nothing that they propose to do will be withheld from them.

Come, let Us go down and there confuse their language, that they may not understand one another's speech."

Genesis 11:4-7, NKJV

God recognized the potential of a unified team, even when that team was not fulfilling a divine purpose. The end of verse 6 in the *NLT* reads, "Nothing they set out to do will be impossible for them!"

What if believers operated in the same type of common language and unified purpose? This is why Paul admonished the Corinthians to " all speak the same thing, and that there be no divisions among you, but that you be perfectly joined together in the same mind and in the same judgment" (1 Corinthians 1:10, *NKJV*).

The idol-makers described by the prophet Isaiah are another example of a unified team.

Everyone helped his neighbor, and said to his brother, "Be of good courage!"

So the craftsman encouraged the goldsmith; He who smooths with the hammer inspired him who strikes the anvil, saying,

"It is ready for the soldering"; Then he fastened it with pegs, that it might not totter.

Isaiah 41:6-7 NLT

These workers celebrated each other's contributions. I can almost picture them giving each other high five's as each one used his respective skills in helping to build a first-class idol. When I first realized exactly what Isaiah is describing, a certain frustration hit me and I thought to myself, *If workers can be that unified and enthusiastic while building dumb idols, how much more should the Church—the Body of Christ—be unified and enthusiastic in our work for God upon the earth?*

Remember, even though teamwork has often been corrupted and used for ungodly purposes, teamwork itself was originally God's idea. Teamwork comes from God's own nature—from the intrinsic unity and functioning of the Trinity. So it's not uncommon at all to see good teams functioning in the Bible.

- Moses had a team that worked with him. Members included Joshua, Aaron, Hur, the elders, and those who took part in building the Tabernacle.

- David had a team of advisors and "The Mighty Men of David." David's Dream Team began with an unlikely group. First Samuel 22:2 says, "And everyone who was in distress, everyone who was in debt, and everyone who was discontented gathered to him. So he became captain over them" (*NKJV*). And yet, it was from this rag-tag group that David's Mighty Men emerged—those whose strength, courage, and commitment enabled David's kingdom to be established and through whom great exploits were done.

- Jesus had a team of disciples that He trained to be His representatives and to carry on His work. Though they ultimately provided leadership and ministry to the early Church, they served very practically during Jesus' ministry (arranging meals, lodging, and transportation, paying taxes, handling His finances...).

- Paul promoted and demonstrated teamwork throughout his ministry. He worked with Barnabas, Mark, Silas, Timothy, Titus, and several others. Second Corinthians 9:5 refers to an "advance team" that Paul sent to Corinth prior to one of his own visits there (*MSG*).

Solomon expressed the value of teamwork when he said, "Two people are better off than one, for they can help each other succeed. If one person falls, the other can reach out and help. But someone who falls alone is in real trouble" (Ecclesiastes 4:9-10, *NLT*). In Judges 18:28, the isolated town of Laish was destroyed when attacked because "there was no one to rescue the people, for they lived a great distance from Sidon and had no allies nearby" (*NLT*). Scripture communicates time and again that isolation is not good and that it can be downright dangerous. The divine remedy? Psalm 68:6 says that "God sets the solitary in families" (*NKJV*).

Elijah was powerfully called and anointed by God, but he had a glaring vulnerability in his life—he was isolated. He served God, but he served God alone. Great miracles happened, but when intense pressure came and he needed a community of faith around him, there was no one from whom he could draw strength. He had not built committed relationships in the good times and when the crisis came, he knew of no recourse but to run, and to run alone. Debilitating fear and an overwhelming despair overtook him. Fortunately, God led him to Elisha, and he finished his ministry with a sense of teamwork and companionship.

In more modern times, John Alexander Dowie stands out as a minister who had great potential but became badly sidetracked. Isolation contributed significantly to severe problems for Dowie. Gordon Lindsay spoke of Dowie's "habit of taking no counsel with others on important matters." Lindsay further wrote,

"...at last [Dowie] came to the place where he confided in no one but himself, and gradually, he assumed the same complex that Elijah had—a feeling that there was no one left on earth that contended for the true faith, but he himself. Such was an unfortunate mistake, for it cut him off from the counsel of others—a most serious circumstance. For God has ordained that ministers as members of the Body of Christ should be open to advice one of another. In the Early Church, they did not just depend on revelations. When important circumstances developed, which required that a vital judgment be made, the apostles and elders came together in a body and consulted together, and arrived at an official decision. Dr. Dowie made all the decisions, and consulted no one except in subordinate matters. He thus deprived himself of valuable counsel, and removed from before him the ordinary restraints that might have checked him in the making of a rash decision."[11]

---

[11]Gordon Lindsay, *John Alexander Dowie*, Christ for the Nations, Inc., Dallas, TX 1980, 197-198

Addressing the issue of personal seclusion, Michael G. Moriarty wrote, "In evangelical individualism people think of their personal relationship with God in isolation ('Just me and Jesus') and forge their destiny apart from any church authority. While holding relatively low opinions of history, tradition, and the church, they turn to the experiences of self and isolate themselves from their brothers and sisters in the faith. True spirituality is perverted as it becomes a quest for inner stimulation rather than growth in biblical knowledge and the application of truth in community. Healthy Christians do not live in isolation!"[12]

The author of the Book of Hebrews encourages an atmosphere of teamwork among believers when he writes, "Let's see how inventive we can be in encouraging love and helping out, not avoiding worshiping together as some do but spurring each other on, especially as we see the big Day approaching" (10:24-25, *MSG*).

Not Just a Team, But a *Determined* Team

Every sports fan knows that it's one thing to have a team; it's another thing to have a team that is prepared, finessed, and relentless in its pursuit of victory. Successful athletes share several common traits, whether they compete in an individual or team sport, and some of these traits are addressed in the New Testament.

> *Don't you realize that in a race everyone runs, but only one person gets the prize? So run to win!*
>
> *All athletes are disciplined in their training. They do it to*

---

[12]Taken from *The Perfect 10* by Michael G. Moriarty, Copyright © 1999. Used by permission of Zondervan. www.zondervan.com

win a prize that will fade away, but we do it for an eternal prize.

So I run with purpose in every step. I am not just shadow-boxing.

I discipline my body like an athlete, training it to do what it should. Otherwise, I fear that after preaching to others I myself might be disqualified.

1 Corinthians 9:24-27, NLT

The phrase "run to win" in verse 24 means *to take eagerly, to seize, and to possess.* Check source for verbatim and check to be sure the citation is formatted correctly.] Paul did not advocate a passive, laid back Christian life. Rather, he likened it to a race that involved discipline, training, purpose, self-control, and a prize to be sought. In the Christian race, we are not competing against each other; we're not trying to out-do one another. Rather, we are competing against our own potential and endeavoring to fulfill our particular callings effectively.

Paul noted that athletes compete for a prize that is temporary and fleeting. However, the spiritual athlete—the devoted follower of Jesus Christ—is pursuing a reward that will never fade away, what Paul calls "an eternal prize."

Paul uses athletic imagery again in Second Timothy 2:5: "…if anyone competes in athletics, he is not crowned unless he competes according to the rules" (*NKJV*). Believers today sometimes don't want to hear about "rules," assuming that rules are an expression of legalism. However, there are certainly principles that govern success and failure when it comes to serving God, just like there are principles that govern the outcome of a team's performance in a sporting event.

As Paul concludes his last epistle (2 Timothy), there are two outstanding issues worth noting. First, he describes the conclusion of his ministry using rich, athletic imagery.

> *I have fought the good fight, I have finished the race, and I have remained faithful.*
>
> *And now the prize awaits me—the crown of righteousness, which the Lord, the righteous Judge, will give me on the day of his return. And the prize is not just for me but for all who eagerly look forward to his appearing.*
>
> *2 Timothy 4:7-8, NLT*

Second, knowing that he'll soon be in Heaven, Paul somewhat nostalgically mentions friends and teammates in ministry with whom he had labored at various times in his journey (2 Timothy 4:9-21):

- **Timothy:** Paul asks that Timothy, his son in the faith, come to him.

- **Demas:** Once a faithful assistant, Demas had abandoned Paul.

- **Crescens and Titus:** Both are off on other ministry assignments.

- **Luke:** Paul's abiding, faithful friend

- **Mark:** A once-strained relationship between them, Mark is now profitable to Paul.

- **Tychicus:** Paul had sent him to Ephesus.

- **Priscilla and Aquila:** Paul called them "my fellow workers in Christ Jesus" and said that they had risked their own necks for his life (Romans 16:3)

- **Onesiphorus and his household:** Paul beautifully describes the comfort and encouragement this friend brought him on more than one occasion (2 Timothy 1:16-18)

- **Erastus:** Stayed in Corinth

- **Trophimus:** Formerly unable to travel with Paul due to illness, he was in Miletus

- **Eubulus, Pudens, Linus, Claudia, and others.**

Paul was no lone ranger, nor was he a "one-man show." It must have been a poignant experience for Paul to remember and write these names. For some he felt great gratitude, but he probably felt sorrow over Demas' departure, and perhaps concern over the illness of Trophimus. It is evident, though, that Paul cultivated and maintained deep friendships and strategic working relationships. He was a team player and always sought to promote a team approach to ministry.

Paul saw himself as a spiritual athlete who would be rewarded for his efforts. Further, he reminded us that we all have the potential to receive the same type of prize. There's a fight we've been called to fight, and a race we've been called to run. We need the same God who empowered Paul, and we need the same kind of teamwork that Paul valued.

Jesus the Champion

The author of Hebrews encourages us to engage wholeheartedly in the "faith marathon," and to realize that Jesus is the great spiritual athlete that we must emulate and follow.

> *Therefore, since we are surrounded by such a huge crowd of witnesses to the life of faith, let us strip off every weight that slows us down, especially the sin that so easily trips us up. And let us run with endurance the race God has set before us.*
>
> *We do this by keeping our eyes on **Jesus, the champion** who initiates and perfects our faith… [emphasis mine].*
>
> *Hebrews 12:1-2, NLT*

The *New King James Version* renders verse 2 as "Jesus, the author and finisher of our faith." Various commentaries render the word "author" as:

- Leader[13]

- Prince-Captain[14]

- Author[15]

- Pioneer[16]

- Trailblazer[17]

- Chief Leader[18]

---

[13]Hebrews. Ed. H. D. M. Spence-Jones. The Pulpit Commentary. London; New York: Funk & Wagnalls Company, 1909.
[14]Robert Jamieson, A. R. Fausset and David Brown. *Commentary Critical and Explanatory on the Whole Bible* Oak Harbor, WA: Logos Research Systems, Inc., 1997
[15]Ibid.
[16]Paul Ellingworth, and Eugene Albert Nida. *A Handbook on the Letter to the Hebrews. UBS Handbook Series.*(New York: United Bible Societies, 1994).
[17]Warren W. Wiersbe. *Wiersbe's Expository Outlines on the New Testament* (Wheaton, IL: Victor Books, 1992).
[18]Kenneth S. Wuest *Wuest's Word Studies from the Greek New Testament: For the English Reader.*(Grand Rapids: Eerdmans, 1997).

- Initiator[19]

- Originator[20]

- Founder (*ESV*)

- Source (*HCSB*)

Greek scholar, Marvin R. Vincent expands on the idea of Jesus as the Author of our faith as follows: "In himself he furnished the perfect development, the supreme example of faith, and in virtue of this he is the leader of the whole believing host in all time."[21] These various insights make me appreciate Jesus as the Champion of faith !

There are many metaphors applied to the Lord Jesus. He is the Good Shepherd; He is the Light of the World; He is the Bread of Life. All of these are wonderful and worthy of detailed study. But in this book we are focusing on Jesus as the Captain of a Championship Team. He was a member of the glorious Trinity before the universe was ever created and now, in addition, He is also the Captain of a new team—the Body of Christ—a team of which we are a part, and one that He is leading to great exploits and accomplishments.

But Jesus is not simply the Author and Champion of our faith; He's also the Perfecter and the Finisher of our faith. We know that Jesus is not simply committed to getting us started, but He's also determined to see us through

---

[19]Ed. D. A. Carson, R. T. France, J. A. Motyer and G. J. Wenham. *New Bible Commentary: 21st Century Edition*. 4th ed. (Leicester, England; Downers Grove, IL: Inter-Varsity Press, 1994).

[20]Warren W. Wiersbe *The Bible Exposition Commentary*. (Wheaton, IL: Victor Books, 1996).

[21]Marvin Richardson Vincent. *Vincent's Word Studies in the New Testament*. (New York: Charles Scribner's Sons, 1887).

to the very end. Wuest says the word "finisher" is from the Greek word te-leioo which means 'to carry through completely, to finish, to make perfect or complete.'"[22] Jesus will never quit on us, so let's never quit on Him!

In the previous chapter, we saw where Jesus prayed for us. He wanted (and still desires today) that we all would be one—united in teamwork—just as He and the Father are one. In the chapters that follow we are going to study the traits of championship teams. We'll focus on traits that Jesus himself exhibited, and we'll also see how these same characteristics have contributed to championship performances in various athletic endeavors. Paul used natural sports examples to illustrate spiritual truths, and we're going to as well. The remainder of the book will focus on a single trait that corresponds with each letter of the word *Champions*:

C: Composure

H: Humility

A: Authenticity

M: Motivation

P: Persistence

I: Interdependence

O: Obscurity

N: Nobility

S: Strategy

---

[22]Kenneth S. Wuest *Wuest's Word Studies from the Greek New Testament: For the English Reader*. (Grand Rapids: Eerdmans, 1997).

Quotes Worth Remembering

"Though I don't like the crew, I won't sink the ship. In fact, in time of storm I'll do my best to save it. You see, we are all in this craft and must sink or swim together."

- Daniel Defoe

"The way a team plays as a whole determines its success. You may have the greatest bunch of individual stars in the world, but if they don't play together, the club won't be worth a dime."

- Babe Ruth

"Teamwork is the ability to work together toward a common vision. The ability to direct individual accomplishment toward organizational objectives. It is the fuel that allows common people to attain uncommon results."

- Andrew Carnegie

"We realized that no one of us could be as good as all of us playing unselfishly."

- Bill Bradley

"If you want to go fast, go alone. If you want to go far, go as a team."

- African Proverb

Questions for Reflection and Discussion

1. Reread Isaiah 41:6-7 on page 36. How are you doing in encouraging your team members and celebrating their accomplishments? Can your team improve in this area?

2. Discuss the connection between the great leaders in the Bible and their teams. How did they work together to accomplish their goals and objectives?

3. What tends to happen when people are isolated in their lives and even in their work for God?

4. How does the New Testament use athletic imagery to describe the Christian life and ministry? What do you think are the parallels?

5. Review the five Quotes Worth Remembering. Which of these quotes speaks the most to you, and how does it specifically impact you?

CHAPTER THREE

Champions Maintain Composure

"Never be in a hurry; do everything quietly and in a calm spirit. Do not lose your inner peace for anything whatsoever, even if your whole world seems upset."

- Saint Francis de Sales

What is composure? It is defined as a serene, self-controlled state of mind; calmness; tranquility.[23] A person who is composed is free from agitation and is collected, coolheaded, undisturbed, unruffled, and unshaken.[24] Simply put, composure is keeping one's cool under pressure.

Composure pays great dividends, not just on the sports field but also in every area of life. Rudolph Giuliani, the former mayor of New York City, said, "My father used to say to me, 'Whenever you get into a jam, whenever you get into a crisis or an emergency...become the calmest person in the room and you'll be able to figure your way out of it.'"

Composure on the Diamond

When baseball executive Branch Rickey was looking to bring the first African American baseball player into the Major Leagues, he knew it would cause significant turmoil due to racist mentalities. He realized the athlete

---

[23]www.dictionary.reference.com, s.v. "composure."
[24]www.merriam-webster.com, s.v. "composed."

who demolished the race barrier would not only have to possess excellent skills, but he would also have to possess great mental toughness and discipline as well. Rickey told Jackie Robinson, "I'm looking for a ballplayer with enough guts not to fight back."[25]

Rickey realized that opposing fans and players would target Robinson and persecute him unfairly and that Robinson would need great depth of character to stay focused and not let the harassment get to him. If opponents could distract him, they would lessen his performance on the field. Rickey understood the principle that Winston Churchill articulated: "You will never reach your destination if you stop and throw stones at every dog that barks."

Composure on the Soccer Field

As I've traveled internationally, I've been amazed at the level of intensity and excitement that accompanies the World Cup. Held every four years, it is the largest and most watched sporting event in the world. Football (what Americans consider "soccer") teams representing thirty-two nations vie to be called the best in the world.

In one World Cup final, two European teams were playing the championship match, and the game ended in a 1-1 tie. In overtime, one player "trash talked" the star player of the other team and insulted his sister. The recipient of the verbal barb lost his cool, head-butted the opposing player in retaliation, and was ejected from the game. With their star player expelled, the team was at a disadvantage and ended up losing the game.

---

[25]Dr. Criswell Freeman, *The Wisdom of Old Time Baseball* (Nashville, TN, Walnut Grove Press, 1996), 86.

A person may be an outstandingly talented player, but if he can't keep his composure and stay focused on playing the game, he'll be more inclined to make mental errors, be more vulnerable to self-implosion, and can undermine the success of the entire team. This is why Oliver Wendell Holmes said, "Have the courage to act instead of react."

Composure on the Basketball Court

NBA great Walt Frazier said, "My definition of discipline is for a player to put his team first and to play under control at all times." He went on to give a great example of this. "Phil Chenier of the Baltimore Bullets once accidentally punched me in the back of the neck—he was trying to strike Bradley but missed and hit me—and the ref called the foul on me for some reason. I didn't yell at the ref or retaliate by throwing a punch at Chenier. I knew what he did wasn't intentional. Even if he did punch me intentionally, I wouldn't have gone after him. I never got into any altercation on the court. Why should I? I'm not going to act with folly because someone else did something to me. When a player keeps a calm demeanor on the court, it's easier for his ability to shine. The best response to an opposing player's physical or psychological tactics is to keep cool and come right back at him with the force of your game, not your fists... I took it to Chenier and scored eight baskets in a row."[26]

Composure in the Life of the Believer

Spiritually and biblically speaking, how significant is composure in the life of a believer? In the life of a ministry team? There are some great men

---

[26]Walt Frazier, *The Game Within the Game*, (New York, NY, Hyperion, 2006), 15-16.

of God who lost their cool. These moments of weakness were not their finest moments.

- Moses lost his cool, struck the rock, and lost the privilege of going into the Promised Land (Numbers 20:7-12; Psalm 106:32-33).

- Elijah lost his cool, panicked, and fled in fear from Jezebel's threat (1 Kings 19:1-3).

- Jonah lost his cool, became angry, expressed a desire to die, and pouted when God forgave the Ninevites (Jonah 4:1-3).

- Peter lost his cool and cut off the ear of the high priest's servant in the Garden of Gethsemane (John 18:10).

- James and John lost their cool and wanted to call down fire on a city (Luke 9:51-56).

- Paul lost his cool and called the high priest a "whitewashed wall" (Acts 23:1-5).

- Euodia and Syntyche lost their cool and had a falling out with each other, threatening the unity of the church (Philippians 4:2-3).

Peter not only lost his cool in the garden, but he also had a history of impulsivity. Peter was often very quick to blurt out his thoughts or opinions without having much of a "filter." For example, when Jesus explained that His future path involved crucifixion, "Peter took Him aside and began to rebuke Him, saying, 'Far be it from You, Lord; this shall not happen to You!'" (Matthew 16:22, *NKJV*). Part of composure is knowing when to keep your mouth closed. Every thought that comes to your mind isn't best spoken. Count to ten. Take a deep breath. Think before you speak, and sometimes it's best to keep your thoughts to yourself.

If you've ever had a problem with maintaining composure, it's good to know that God helped and mightily used people who had problems keeping theirs, but it is important that we allow Him to mature and develop us in this area. In reality, growing in composure is essentially synonymous with growing in the fruit of the Spirit (Galatians 5:22-23). It's what happens when we submit our will and temperament to the transforming power of God's Spirit and Word.

When people lose their composure, their focus is disrupted; they get sidetracked and react carnally to external irritants. Composure exists when your purpose and priorities are bigger to you than your pressures and problems. Composure keeps you steady, grounded, and on track. People with composure "keep it together" because they see that the big-ness of what they are called to do is bigger than the pettiness of all that would detract and distract from the fulfilling of their high purpose.

In my book *Qualified*, I shared the following admonition: "Don't allow a misbehaving person to drag you down to their level. Here are some important things to remember:

- Don't let someone else's problem become your problem.

- Don't let someone else's carnality bring out your carnality.

- Don't let someone else's sin get you into sin.

- Don't live your life reacting to someone else's 'flesh' problem. Live your life responding to the power of God's love."[27]

A Drama-Free Zone

When team members are committed to keeping their composure, the team is much more likely to enjoy a "drama-free zone." What is present in a high drama atmosphere?

- Over-reacting, making mountains out of mole hills

- Immaturity, pettiness, and strife

- Whining, pouting, and self-pity

- Tantrums and passive aggressive behavior

- Gossip and back-biting

- People who are easily offended and reactionary

- Displays of temper and out-of-control emotions

- Disrespect toward others

- High-maintenance individuals

- Reckless speech

- Lack of self-control

- Self-centeredness and self-absorption

Working together without excessive drama does not mean that team members stuff their feelings or never share their frustrations. In reality, open, honest, respectful, and mature communication that identifies and resolves conflicts is key to keeping pressure from building up and causing an

---

[27]Tony Cooke, Qualified: *Serving God with Integrity and Finishing Your Course with Honor* (Tulsa, OK, Harrison House, 2012), 238-239.

explosion. Healthy teams hold each other accountable and are not afraid to "speak the truth in love" (Ephesians 4:15). When team members have truly submitted themselves to one another and to the good of the team, the "iron sharpens iron" (Proverbs 27:17) principle comes into play and there can be some healthy sparks without having unnecessary drama. In healthy teams, members talk *to* one another, not *about* one another.

Keeping drama to a minimum also does not mean that the team fails to recognize or support a member who is going through adversity. On the contrary, good team members care deeply for one another and really do "bear one another's burdens, and so fulfill the law of Christ" (Galatians 6:2, *NKJV*). In fact, Jesus said to His own disciples, "You've stuck with me through thick and thin" (Luke 22:28, *MSG*). Teams are not comprised of disengaged, emotionless robots; rather, team members encourage and support one another through the challenges of life.

Composure and Qualifications for Leadership

In First Timothy 3:1-7, Paul lists several qualifications for bishops—those in spiritual leadership. It's amazing how many of these traits are related to composure. Let's consider just a few of these qualities:

- **Blameless:** This refers to a virtuous person, a man of good character. There is nothing in this man's life that would be grounds for any legitimate accusation against him, nothing that would cause others to stumble or bring any type of reproach upon Christ or the Church. Someone who is always flying off the handle and losing his composure would hardly be known as blameless.

- **Temperate:** This term comes from a word meaning "sober" or "calm in judgment." A temperate person is well balanced, self-controlled, and not given to impulsivity or excesses. This person is also objective and thoughtful and does not act rashly.

- **Sober-Minded:** This trait describes a person who is "in control of himself, not given to anger, personal ambition, or passions. He is to be sensible and in charge of his life."[28] Furthermore, the term "suggests that he knows the value of things and does not cheapen the ministry or the Gospel message by foolish behavior."[29] A sober-minded person is serious, steady, and stable.

- **Of Good Behavior:** A person who is characterized by good behavior will have a well-ordered life and be dignified. He or she will not be given to excesses, disorder, carelessness, or slack.

- **Not Violent:** This person is not a quick-tempered hothead who is controlled by emotions and inclined to act angrily. A spiritual leader is not to be contentious.

- **Gentle:** A gentle person is kind, fair, just, and considerate of others. He is also moderate and patient toward people.

- **Not Quarrelsome:** These people are not bullies; they don't go around with a chip on their shoulder. A quarrelsome person is argumentative and looking to pick a fight.

- **Has a Good Testimony Among Those Who Are Outside:** This

---

[28]Knute Larson, *I & II Thessalonians, I & II Timothy, Titus, Philemon, Holman New Testament Commentary* (Nashville, TN: Broadman & Holman Publishers, 2000), 183.
[29]Warren W. Wiersbe, *The Bible Exposition Commentary* (Wheaton, IL: Victor Books, 1996). 1 Ti 3:2d.

phrase literally means "a good witness." This leader's character and integrity is such that he is widely respected in the community; his reputation is solidly positive.

While you may not aspire to be a bishop or in fulltime ministry, we are all called to be spiritual leaders—whether in the home, workplace, or community—and these traits listed in First Timothy 3 should be evident in all of us as we mature in Christ.

Jesus and Composure

Who is the greatest example of composure? Jesus, the Champion! In the face of lies, vicious attacks, and even crucifixion, He kept his composure like no other. He was not moved by persecution, pressure, or pain because His life was consumed with a purpose. His face was set like flint to do the Father's will. Isaiah had even prophesied Jesus' focus and self-control.

The Lord God has opened My ear; and I was not rebellious, nor did I turn away.

I gave My back to those who struck Me, and My cheeks to those who plucked out the beard; I did not hide My face from shame and spitting.

For the Lord God will help Me; Therefore I will not be disgraced; Therefore I have set My face like a flint, and I know that I will not be ashamed.

Isaiah 50:5-7, NKJV

He was oppressed and He was afflicted, yet He opened not His mouth; He was led as a lamb to the slaughter, and as a sheep before its shearers is silent, so He opened not His mouth.

Isaiah 53:7, NKJV

Instead of reacting to the hatred of those who crucified Him, Jesus said, "Father, forgive them, for they know not what they do" (Luke 23:34, *NKJV*). Jesus was disciplined and consistently responded from divine love; He did not haphazardly react to the carnal issues of others.

Composure does not mean that a person is a robot. Jesus had composure, and yet He experienced the full spectrum of human emotion; He rejoiced, grieved, and even experienced anger. Jesus did not lose His composure when He cleared out the moneychangers from the temple. He was in control of His anger; His anger was not in control of Him. The Bible says, "Be angry, and do not sin" (Ephesians 4:26, *NKVJ*).

Also keep in mind that composure is not the same as passivity. Composure occurs when a person is so consumed with a compelling purpose that he does not allow himself to be ruled by irritations, frustrations, and offenses. Team members who keep their cool under pressure—who maintain composure—are able to stay focused and free from distractions that will undermine their performance and reduce their contribution to the team effort.

A Team Prayer Concerning Composure

Father, thank You that You are helping us grow in composure and stability. As we serve You and work with one another, I ask You to help us stay focused on the things that really matter to You. We surrender to You any fleshly tendencies we have toward drama or over-reacting, and we determine before You that we will not live in an agitated, unsettled state. Help us to walk in peace and to express peace toward one another. Thank You for the fruit of the Spirit growing in our lives, and thank You that You help us not be distracted by petty things but to steadily apply ourselves toward the work of Your Kingdom. In Jesus' name we pray, amen.

Quotes Worth Remembering

"Those who have accomplished the greatest results are those...who never grow excited or lose self-control, but are always calm, self-possessed, patient and polite."

- Booker T. Washington

"If you can keep your head when all about you are losing theirs and blaming it on you...Yours is the earth and everything that's in it."

- Rudyard Kipling

"There has never been, and cannot be, a good life, without self-control."

- Leo Tolstoy

"Leadership is a matter of having people look at you and gain confidence, seeing how you react. If you're in control, they're in control."

- Tom Landry

"I've trained all my life not to be distracted by distractions."

- Nik Wallenda

Questions for Reflection and Discussion

1. Identify someone you know who maintains his or her composure

well. Describe how you've seen composure operate in this person's life and the benefits it produces.

2. Identify a time when you were tempted to lose your composure but did not. How did this benefit you?

3. Identify a time when you lost your composure. Did it create problems? How did you recover?

4. What are some practical ways that a composed team functions—what happens when composure is part of the team culture?

5. What does a team look like and what happens when composure is absent from the team culture?

6. In what ways can you and your team grow in the area of maintaining composure, and how would this bring improvement to the work all of you are doing?

7. Review the five Quotes Worth Remembering. Which of these quotes speaks the most to you, and how does it specifically impact you?

Group Exercise: Beyond Composure

For the letter "C" in *Champions*, I chose "composure." There are other words, though, that begin with the letter "C" that have to do with great teamwork and championship performances. How are you doing and how is your team doing in regard to the following?

Commitment: Are team members committed to the vision and mission?

Competence: Are team members operating skillfully and seeking to increase their skill levels?

Chemistry: Is there good team chemistry? If not, what can be done to improve it?

Communication: Are team members communicating well with one another?

Discuss these areas and do some self-assessment with other members of the team. Acknowledge and affirm the areas where the team is doing well. Also discuss what can be done to strengthen any areas needing improvement.

CHAPTER FOUR

Champions Embrace Humility

"There are people with a lot more talent than I have who have been weeded out of the league because they couldn't put their egos aside to fill a role."[30]

- Kurt Rambis

In a vital game, a premier basketball team was trailing by one point with a couple of seconds left on the clock. The coach called time out and designed a play. They would get one final shot and the coach knew that the other team would be expecting their star player to take it, so he assigned him to be a decoy. Someone would fake passing to him, allowing another player on the team to be free for the score. When the star player realized he would not be taking the clutch shot, he sat on the bench and refused to play those final, critical seconds. The other player made the shot, which resulted in a win for the team. However, the team floundered in subsequent games, and many blamed the star player's attitudes and actions for the decline in the team's morale and performance.

Pride causes people to exalt themselves above others, to be unwilling to adapt or adjust, and to be rigid and inflexible. Humility, on the other hand, leads people to seek the welfare of the whole team, rejoice in the accom-

[30]Dr. Criswell Freeman, The Book of Basketball Wisdom, Nashville, TN. Walnut Grove Press, 1997, Page 70.

plishments of one's teammates, and to do whatever it takes to contribute toward the team's success, regardless of whether theirs is a leading or a supporting role. Humility enables a player to see that "the goal is more important than the role" and that "we" is more important than "me."

Jesus is the ultimate team player! His humility and consequent obedience is conveyed beautifully in the Book of Philippians.

> *You must have the same attitude that Christ Jesus had.*
>
> *Though he was God, he did not think of equality with God as something to cling to.*
>
> *Instead, he gave up his divine privileges; he took the humble position of a slave and was born as a human being. When he appeared in human form,*
>
> *he humbled himself in obedience to God and died a criminal's death on a cross.*
>
> *Therefore, God elevated him to the place of highest honor and gave him the name above all other names,*
>
> *that at the name of Jesus every knee should bow, in heaven and on earth and under the earth,*
>
> *and every tongue confess that Jesus Christ is Lord, to the glory of God the Father.*
>
> *Philippians 2:5-11, NLT*

The Message renders a portion of this passage, "When the time came, [Jesus] set aside the privileges of deity and took on the status of a slave, became human! Having become human, he stayed human. It was an incredibly humbling process. He didn't claim special privileges. Instead, he lived a selfless, obedient life and then died a selfless, obedient death."

Jesus humbled Himself.

Those are some of the most powerful words ever spoken. Had Jesus not done so—had He not humbly embraced the role of a servant—God's plan to save mankind could have never materialized. Jesus did not complain that His assignment required Him to obediently walk dusty roads and to work within a human framework that involved hunger, thirst, weariness, and eventually death. We are called to follow the same example of humility that Jesus exhibited—the teamwork that He displayed within the working of His Team, the Trinity.

Humility is not a pretense; it is not a superficial, self-deprecating attitude that is merely a ploy to *appear* humble. As Fred Smith said, "Humility is not denying the power you have. It is realizing that the power comes through you, not from you." True humility recognizes God as the source of every blessing and strength in one's life and produces a submitted, yielded, and obedient life.

Gary Inrig wrote, "A large group of European pastors came to one of D.L. Moody's Northfield Bible Conferences in Massachusetts in the late 1800s. Following the European custom of the time, each guest put his shoes outside his room to be cleaned by the hall servants overnight. But of course this was America and there were no hall servants.

"Walking the dormitory halls that night, Moody saw the shoes and determined not to embarrass his brothers. He mentioned the need to some ministerial students who were there, but met with only silence or pious excuses. Moody returned to the dorm, gathered up the shoes, and, alone in his room, the world's only famous evangelist began to clean and polish the shoes. Only the unexpected arrival of a friend in the midst of the work revealed the secret.

"When the foreign visitors opened their doors the next morning, their shoes were shined. They never knew by whom. Moody told no one, but his friend told a few people, and during the rest of the conference, different men volunteered to shine the shoes in secret. Perhaps the episode is a vital insight into why God used D. L. Moody as He did. He was a man with a servant's heart and that was the basis of his true greatness."[31]

A Humble Champion Is Selfless

A player with true humility is not self-promoting; instead, he will take on whatever role is necessary to help the team win. NBA great Bill Walton said, "The nicest thing people ever said about me as a basketball player was that I made the players around me better. To me, there's no higher compliment."[32] That is a refreshing attitude.

Jesus spoke of the Father, saying, "I always do those things that please Him" (John 8:29, *NKJV*). We also read that "Christ didn't live to please himself" (Romans 15:3, *NLT*). Jesus taught us that His assignment was to be a servant for the benefit of others, and He taught us that we are to follow in His footsteps.

---

[31]Gary Inrig, *A Call to Excellence,* (Wheaton, IL, Victor Books, a division of SP Publishing, 1985), 98.
[32]Dr. Criswell Freeman, The Book of Basketball Wisdom, Nashville, TN, Walnut Grove Press, 1997, Page 66.

...Whoever wants to be a leader among you must be your servant,

and whoever wants to be first among you must become your slave.

For even the Son of Man came not to be served but to serve others and to give his life as a ransom for many.

Matthew 20:26-28, NLT

At the Last Supper, the disciples got into one of their common arguments about which of them was the greatest (Luke 22:24). In the midst of their ego-based bickering, Jesus did something remarkable. He got a basin and towel, and washed all of their feet—He did the work of a servant. Afterward, He exhorted them.

You call Me Teacher and Lord, and you say well, for so I am.

If I then, your Lord and Teacher, have washed your feet, you also ought to wash one another's feet.

For I have given you an example, that you should do as I have done to you.

Most assuredly, I say to you, a servant is not greater than his master; nor is he who is sent greater than he who sent him.

If you know these things, blessed are you if you do them.

John 13:13-17, NKJV

Peter was one of those present at the table that night, one of those whose feet were washed by Jesus, and he later wrote, "Yes, all of you be submissive to one another, and be clothed with humility"... "humble yourselves under the mighty hand of God, that He may exalt you in due time" (1 Peter 5:5-6, *NKJV*).

Selflessness may be the Kingdom standard, but it is not necessarily common, even among believers. When Paul was describing the uniqueness of Timothy, one of Timothy's distinguishing characteristics was the fact that, unlike others, he was not self-seeking (Philippians 2:21). Considering this, I did a quick overview of the Bible to see what exactly it is that people seek. I searched through Scripture to complete the statement, "People seek their own _____. " These are some of the insights from Scripture:

- **People seek their own glory**

To seek one's own glory is not glory" (Proverbs 25:27, *NKJV*).

- **People seek their own greatness**

"Do you seek great things for yourself? Do not seek them…" (Jeremiah 45:5, *NKJV*).

- **People seek their own will**

"I do not seek my own will but the will of the Father who sent Me" (John 5:30, *NKJV*).

- **People seek their own convenience**

"Those of us who are strong and able in the faith need to step in and lend a hand to those who falter, and not just do what is most convenient for us. Strength is for service, not status. Each one of us needs to look after the good of the people around us, asking ourselves, 'How can I help?'" (Romans 15:1-2, *MSG*).

- **People seek their own profit**

"...not seeking my own profit, but the profit of many, that they may be saved" (1 Corinthians 10:33, *NKJV*).

- **People seek their own good**

"Nobody should seek his own good, but the good of others" (1 Corinthians 10:24, *NIV*).

- **People seek their own popularity**

"Do I seek to please men? For if I still pleased men, I would not be a bondservant of Christ" (Galatians 1:10, *NKJV*).

- **People seek their own interests.**

"Each of you should look not only to your own interests, but also to the interests of others" (Philippians 2:4, *NIV*).

With all of these admonitions, it's no wonder that Paul says that love does not seek its own (1 Corinthians 13:5), and that church leaders must not be self-willed (Titus 1:7). The word "self-willed" that Paul uses here means *self-pleasing, self-loving,* and *one who is dominated by self-interest and is inconsiderate of others.* If we're going to be good team players, our humility should be evident by the fact that we are not rigidly obsessed with our personal preferences.

I heard of a pastor who had made some adjustments in the worship music in the church services; he had added some more contemporary styles to help strengthen their ministry to younger people. After a few months, one of the older ladies in the church approached him after a service and asked to have a word with him, telling him in advance that she wanted to discuss the music. Bracing himself, he expected to hear disapproving words of criticism.

Instead, this kind lady let him know she had noted the change, and said, "Ever since my grandson was born, I've been praying for him to be saved. I've brought him to church periodically, but he's typically not been very interested. However, since you've brought in some of these newer songs, he's a lot more willing to come to church with me, and he's paying more attention. I personally don't like this newer music; I prefer the older songs I'm used to. But if this more modern worship music will help young people like my grandson get saved, then I'm 100% behind these changes."

Selflessness puts the needs of others before our own preferences, and it's an important expression of humility. To put this in basketball terms, we should be just as pleased to lead the team in assists as we would to lead the team in points scored.

A Humble Champion Is Adaptable

There's nothing wrong with having specific gifts or a distinct focus, but there's much to be said in favor of flexibility. In baseball, a "utility player" is one who can play several positions well. In cricket, this type of player is called an "all rounder."

Patrick Ewing, retired center for the New York Knicks and a member of the '92 Dream Team, was describing the importance of adaptability when he said, "The greatest players fit with the team. They play within the team's style, rather than asking the team to change its style."[33] Championship teams are rooted in certain core values, but they adjust in certain areas as necessary in order to accomplish their goals. Former NHL coach Scotty Bowman said, "I found out that if you are going to win games, you had better be ready to adapt."

Kempie Womble, a friend of mine, played offensive tackle for the South Carolina Gamecocks. Their team was excited for the opportunity to play the University of Notre Dame due to the tradition and history of the Irish program. On an attempted pass play, Kempie found himself several feet behind the quarterback who was being tackled by a Notre Dame defender. Right before he went down, the quarterback looked back, saw Kempie, and pitched him the ball.

Remember, Kempie was an offensive tackle, not a running back. It's not his job to run the ball, but Kempie caught it and took off. In his one-and-only carry in his college career, Kempie ran ten yards just to get to the line of scrimmage, and then advanced the ball an additional seven yards before being tackled. He jokes about finishing his collegiate career with the team's highest rushing record—with a seven-yards-per-carry average.

The point is that he had to be flexible. He didn't say, "Running the football is not my responsibility; it's not in my job description." No, Kempie did what the situation required, and he gained important yardage for the benefit

---

[33]Dr. Criswell Freeman, The Book of Basketball Wisdom, Nashville, TN, Walnut Grove Press, 1997, Page 64.

of his team.

When God put His plan to save humanity into action, He exhibited the greatest example of adaptability the world has ever seen—the Incarnation, in which God became man. Thankfully, Jesus did not protest saying, "We've never done it this way before."

The Apostle Paul is another team player who demonstrated adaptability in his approach to ministry.

> *Even though I am a free man with no master, I have become a slave to all people to bring many to Christ.*
>
> *When I was with the Jews, I lived like a Jew to bring the Jews to Christ. When I was with those who follow the Jewish law, I too lived under that law. Even though I am not subject to the law, I did this so I could bring to Christ those who are under the law.*
>
> *When I am with the Gentiles who do not follow the Jewish law, I too live apart from that law so I can bring them to Christ. But I do not ignore the law of God; I obey the law of Christ.*
>
> *When I am with those who are weak, I share their weakness, for I want to bring the weak to Christ. Yes, I try to find common ground with everyone, doing everything I can to save some.*
>
> *I do everything to spread the Good News and share in its blessings.*
>
> *1 Corinthians 9:19-23, NLT*

Paul did not compromise his integrity, but he adjusted his approach in order to reach his audience. You might have a specific ministry, but your methods may need to change at various times as you adapt to a particular situation.

Humility prompts us to adjust, to adapt, and to be flexible. Within the confines of ethics and morality, we are to do whatever it takes to be as effective as possible with the resources we have and the people with whom we work. One of the keys to remaining adaptable is to avoid having a "know-it-all" attitude. Proud people are often very inflexible. Author Eric Hoffer once said, "In times of change learners will inherit the earth, while the learned find themselves beautifully equipped to deal with a world that no longer exists."

Part of adaptability is being able to deal constructively with changes and transitions. We all want to be part of a team where we're comfortable with all the other members, but teams change. People come and go. If you are adaptable, you'll not only stay steady during times of transition, but you'll also make yourself available to do whatever is necessary when things on the team are changing.

A Humble Champion Is Manageable

A humble player is teachable, manageable, and correctable. Babe Ruth, one of the greatest home run hitters of all time, said, "Don't be afraid to take advice. There's always something new to learn."[34] Manageability has to do with one's ability to receive and follow instructions, to follow directions, and even to receive correction and make necessary adjustments. Be-

---

[34]Dr. Criswell Freeman, The Wisdom of Old Time Baseball, Nashville, TN, Walnut Grove Press, 1996, Page 31.

ing manageable is specifically connected to a willingness to cooperate with those in authority.

Several years ago, my wife Lisa and I visited John Wesley's house in London. I saw posted there Wesley's "Rules of an Assistant," written in 1744. One of the twelve points was: "Act in all things not according to your own will but as a son in the Gospel. As such, it is your part to employ your time in a manner which we direct: partly in visiting the flock from house to house (the sick in particular); partly, in such a course of reading, meditation and prayer as we advise from time to time. Above all, if you labor with us in the Lord's vineyard, it is needful you should do that part of the work which we direct, at those times and places which we judge most for his glory." Wesley was looking for people who would follow directions. That seems simple, but many people lack the humility to be truly manageable.

A pastor once told me about a leader in his church that he had to release from his position. The pastor had asked for a simple list regarding the leader's assigned area of responsibility, but the leader never provided the list. When asked, the leader would tell the pastor, "I'm praying about it." A year later, after multiple requests, the pastor felt he had no choice but to relieve that leader of his position. Another leader came to the pastor to let him know he'd made the right decision. The other leader said, "Pastor, you had no choice. The person you let go told me personally, 'I'm not going to give Pastor that list unless the Lord tells me to do it.'" Such a defiant attitude is badly misguided and terribly disruptive to team spirit.

Claiming to be submitted to divine authority while rebelling against delegated natural authority is both prideful and ignorant. Hebrews 13:17 says, "Obey your spiritual leaders, and do what they say. Their work is to watch over your souls, and they are accountable to God. Give them reason to do this with joy and not with sorrow" (*NLT*). While there are times to speak up and stand firm (e.g., when a leader is clearly amoral or asking you to do something unethical), the Bible is clear on the issue: we cannot claim to be humble and teachable if we continually demand our own way and refuse to follow the leadership that's in place—whether at our job or at our place of ministry. Learning to walk in humility will benefit us personally and will help us be the kind of team player that is "champion" material.

A Team Prayer Concerning Humility

Father, we desire with all of our heart to have the same attitude of humility that Jesus had. He did not cling to His privileges, but He took on the role of a servant and lived obediently. We want to be like Jesus. We recognize that every gift and skill we have is from You and that we are merely stewards—not owners—of those gifts. We pray that all we have and all that we are will be used for Your glory. We ask that You will help us be selfless, adaptable, and manageable so that we can work cooperatively and respectfully with one another. In Jesus' name we pray, amen.

Quotes Worth Remembering

"He that falls in love with himself will have no rivals."

- Benjamin Franklin

"The axe cannot boast of the trees it has cut down. It could do nothing but for the woodsman. He made it, he sharpened

it, and he used it."

- Samuel Brengle

"Progress is impossible without change, and those who cannot change their minds cannot change anything."

- George Bernard Shaw

"There are many of us that are willing to do great things for the Lord, but few of us are willing to do little things."

- D.L. Moody

"Well, I think we tried very hard not to be overconfident, because when you get overconfident, that's when something snaps up and bites you."

- Neil Armstrong

Questions for Reflection and Discussion

1. Identify someone you know who exhibits humility. Describe how you've seen humility operate in this person's life and what benefits it produces.

2. Identify a time when you operated in and exhibited humility. What were the benefits?

3. Identify a time when you failed to operate in humility. Did it create problems? How did you recover?

4. What are some practical ways that a humble team functions? What happens when humility is part of the team culture?

5. What does a team look like and what happens when humility is

absent from the team culture?

6. In what ways can you and your team grow in the area of exhibiting humility, and how would this improve the work all of you are doing?

7. Review the five Quotes Worth Remembering. Which of these quotes speaks the most to you and how does it specifically impact you?

Group Exercise: Beyond Humility

For the letter "H" in *Champions*, I chose "humility." There are other words, though, that begin with the letter "H" that have to do with great teamwork and championship performances. How are you doing and how is your team doing in regard to the following?

Honesty: Do team members speak the truth in love to one another?

Honor: Do team members honor, value, and esteem one another?

Hopeful: Do team members have a confident expectation about the future?

Hustle: Are team members giving their best effort?

Discuss these areas and do some self-assessment with other members of the team. Acknowledge and affirm the areas where the team is doing well. Also discuss how improvement can take place in needed areas.

CHAPTER FIVE

Champions Are Authentic

"I believe God made me for a purpose, but he also made me fast! And when I run I feel his pleasure."

- Eric Liddell

A shepherd boy was facing his fiercest test and the greatest opportunity of his young life. Standing before him and the Israelite army was an enemy—a battle-tested warrior named Goliath, a giant of a man and a killing machine. With a confidence that could have only come from God, young David ran toward Goliath and defeated the giant with a rock hurled from his sling. Before the battle, David had refused the king's offer to wear what was undoubtedly the finest armor in Israel.

Then Saul gave David his own armor—a bronze helmet and a coat of mail.

David put it on, strapped the sword over it, and took a step or two to see what it was like, for he had never worn such things before. "I can't go in these," he protested to Saul. "I'm not used to them." So David took them off again.

He picked up five smooth stones from a stream and put them into his shepherd's bag. Then, armed only with his shepherd's staff and sling, he started across the valley to fight the Philistine.

1 Samuel 17:38-40, NLT

David might have *looked* better in Saul's armor, but he probably would have been killed wearing Saul's armor. David had to be true to who he was, and he was wise to use the tools with which he was proficient, that had served him well in the past.

We recognize David's faith in this great victory, but his *authenticity* was also a contributing factor. The word "authentic" is defined as *real or genuine; not copied or false; true and accurate; true to one's own personality, spirit, or character.*[35]

We must never forfeit our principles for the praise of men, surrender our convictions for the sake of convenience, or abandon our values to feed our vanity. We should never forget who God made us to be or abdicate the assignment He has given us to fulfill. If we lose sight of these things, we lose our authenticity and genuineness, becoming play-actors instead of serving God sincerely from the heart.

People sometimes miss God's best because they're busy trying to be something that they're not. Maybe they're trying to impress others or attempting to over-compensate for insecurities. A great example of the importance of being authentic is seen in *Cool Runnings*, the movie about the Jamaican bobsled team that participated in the 1988 Winter Olympics.

The four members of the team were all great sprinters, but none of them had ever participated in winter sports of any kind, so they were at a huge disadvantage. The prospect of hurtling down an ice-covered track at breakneck speeds was intimidating enough to them, but then they started watch-

---

[35]Merriam Webster Dicitonary, s.v. "authentic"

ing some of the other teams—the highly-seasoned Swiss team in particular. They actually started imitating the Swiss team, even in the count to launch (saying "eins, zwei, drei" instead of "one, two, three"). Finally, the team got tired of being intimidated and of trying to act like someone else, and they simply set out to be the best they could be.[36]

In other cases, people start out genuinely enough but lose their bearings—even their identity—over time. If you are familiar with the *Rocky* movies, in which Sylvester Stallone plays Rocky Balboa, you have an idea of what I'm talking about.

In the first movie, Rocky is a gritty, amateur boxer; there's nothing classy or refined about him. When he gets the amazing opportunity to fight the reigning world champ, he begins to train in dimly lit gyms and to run in rough neighborhoods. He wears cheap workout clothes, drinks raw eggs, and punches out sides of beef in a refrigerated meat locker. Rocky's endearing trait is that he is who he is—he's a blue-collar brawler, and he doesn't try to be anything that he's not.

By the time *Rocky 3* rolls around, there is a totally different story. Rocky has defeated Apollo Creed and is basking in the limelight of being the world champion. He's now living in a mansion, driving luxury cars, and wearing the finest clothes. He gets caught up in the fame, the bright lights, and all the media attention; he no longer has the hunger that led him to greatness. You can almost hear Samuel's rebuke to Saul in the background, "When you were little in your own eyes..." (1 Samuel 15:17, *NKJV*).

---

[36]Cool Runnings. Dir. Jon Turteltaub. Buena Vista Pictures Distribution, 1993. Film.

Knowing that Rocky has been lulled into softness over time, his trainer Mickey says to him, "Three years ago you was supernatural. You was hard and you was nasty and you had this cast-iron jaw but then the worst thing happened to you, that could happen to any fighter. You got civilized."[37] After being soundly beaten by Clubber Lang, Rocky goes back to the basics, leaves the glitz and glamour behind, and trains until he once again has "the eye of the tiger." Having shed all of the peripheral hype and reclaimed his authentic self, Rocky regains the title in a rematch against Lang.

King Uzziah is a biblical character—a leader of Israel—who fell into the trap of forgetting his roots. The Bible says that Uzziah "sought God... and as long as he sought the Lord, God made him prosper" (2 Chronicles 26:5, *NKJV*). Uzziah's abundant exploits are catalogued, but then we read, "So his fame spread far and wide, for he was marvelously helped till he became strong. But when he was strong his heart was lifted up, to his destruction, for he transgressed against the LORD his God" (2 Chronicles 26:15-16, *NKJV*).

I remember hearing a staff member from a noted mega-church reflect on the team culture that had developed in the church prior to the senior leader's moral failure. The reflective staff member said, "I guess we'd all gotten a little cocky." Authenticity is related to humility (which we discussed in the last chapter) in that anytime we become arrogant, we will neither be genuine nor express the true character that God designed us to have.

What about us? Do we remember the consecrations we made in our earlier days? Do we remember being willing to pay any price? We prayed,

---

[37] *Rocky III*. Dir. Sylvester Stallone. MGM/UA Entertainment Company, 1982. Film.

"God, I'll go where You want me to go. I'll do what You want me to do. I'll say what You want me to say." Serving God was fresh and exciting. We weren't just going through the motions or the mechanics of ministry; it was genuine and came from a sincere heart. We wanted to glorify God, and we wanted to help people.

Have we maintained that desire? Is ministry now just a performance? Are we just going through the motions? Are we only focused on just getting bills paid and keeping programs going? God, help us have authenticity and be who You made us to be!

God greatly values our authenticity, and it is commended throughout Scripture:

- "God can't stand pious poses, but he delights in genuine prayers" (Proverbs 15:8, *MSG*).
- Romans 12:9 says, "Love from the center of who you are; don't fake it" (*MSG*).
- Paul told the Philippians that Timothy "genuinely cares about your welfare." (Philippians 2:20, *NLT*). Right after that, Paul said, "You know yourselves that Timothy's the real thing" (Philippians 2:20, *MSG*).
- Paul's desire was that all believers be "filled with love that comes from a pure heart, a clear conscience, and genuine faith" (1 Timothy 1:5, *NLT*).
- Peter said, "You must show sincere love to each other as brothers

and sisters. Love each other deeply with all your heart" (1 Peter 1:22, *NLT*).

When the pressures of life build and when the "fear of man" presents itself, we have a choice to make. We can either retreat into hypocrisy or stand in authenticity. Threatened with the possibility of execution, Martin Luther was under pressure to recant and renounce his own writings. He said, "Unless I am convinced by the testimonies of the Holy Scriptures or evident reason...I am bound by the Scriptures...and my conscience has been taken captive to the Word of God, and I am neither able nor willing to recant, since it is neither safe nor right to act against conscience. God help me. Amen."

Unlike Luther, Peter and Barnabas forfeited their authenticity—at least for a short time—in a situation that the Apostle Paul described in Galatians.

> *But when Peter came to Antioch, I had to oppose him to his face, for what he did was very wrong.*
>
> *When he first arrived, he ate with the Gentile Christians, who were not circumcised. But afterward, when some friends of James came, Peter wouldn't eat with the Gentiles anymore. He was afraid of criticism from these people who insisted on the necessity of circumcision.*
>
> *As a result, other Jewish Christians followed Peter's hypocrisy, and even Barnabas was led astray by their hypocrisy.*
>
> *Galatians 2: 11-13, NLT*

Notice that Peter and Barnabas weren't the only ones affected by their retreat into hypocrisy. Other Christians "followed" and were "led astray." It is better for us and for the Body of Christ if we choose to stand in authenticity.

There are times when it takes courage to be authentic and to stand for one's beliefs. We often hear the admonition, "Be yourself." I want to tweak that phrase and encourage you to "be your *best* self!" I've occasionally seen people use the "I'm just being me" or "That's just the way I am" excuse to justify their crass, carnal, undisciplined, and immature behavior. Again, be your *best* self. Be the person that God made you to be. Be the team that God created you to be and tackle the assignment that God has given you. Don't be an imitator of others because if you are, you'll never be anything except second best. Be authentic and let God work through you as He desires.

Back to the Basics

When athletes are "off" and their performance flounders, coaches take the team back to the basics. The team's next several practices are likely to involve reviewing the fundamentals of the game and practicing them over and over. Coaches will have their players practice the basics repeatedly, so that the skills they need to perform in games become second nature to them.

Likewise, in the Church, we need to be ever mindful of the basics of who Jesus has called us to be and what Jesus has called us to do. Are we busy and distracted doing things we were never called to do, and thereby executing poorly or ignoring completely the real priorities that Jesus has for us?

I realize that believers and churches will have certain specific "assignments" from God, targeted outreaches that are to be carried out. I'm fully in favor of those assignments being carried out well. Unfortunately, though, some churches are trying to do so many things that they've become ineffective across the board. It would be better for them to do a few things well than to do many things poorly.

Ineffectiveness is often due to a lack of "pruning." Certain outreaches, programs, and ministries have a "shelf-life" that should be observed. If a particular ministry aim has failed to be useful and fruitful, it either needs to be re-vitalized or discontinued. Jesus said, "He cuts off every branch of mine that doesn't produce fruit, and he prunes the branches that do bear fruit so they will produce even more" (John 15:2, *NLT*). I'm not suggesting arbitrarily and recklessly discontinuing any given program, but neither should we continue ministries just because "we've always done it that way."

As churches and ministries, we sometimes have to ask what it is that God has called *us* to do. We can't do everything, and, again, it's better to do a few things well than several things poorly. So how do we determine what's really important? Most churches will have a mission and/or vision statement that articulates what it is they believe they are supposed to be doing. Even churches that don't have a written statement will have core values, even if they're never officially articulated. Hopefully, what the church emphasizes and focuses its energies on will be grounded in Scripture.

In the summer of 1981, I attended an evangelism conference in Kansas City. During one of the workshops, a speaker addressed major attributes of the Church in the book of Acts, identifying seven traits, each of which began with the Greek letters *kappa* (K) or *delta* (D). Though I don't remember the presenter or the title of the session, I still remember those points. They remind me still today that the Church is not a one-dimensional entity. Any pastor can review this list and ask the question, "How are we doing in emphasizing things that were vital in the life of the early Church?"

Key Characteristics of the Early Church

1. *Kerygma* (Proclamation)

This word can refer to the content of what is preached or the act of preaching itself. *Kerygma* was eventually understood as the initial message proclaimed by the apostles as they introduced unbelievers to Christ. In other words, it was the foundational truth of the Gospel that was proclaimed to persuade individuals to put their faith in and to become followers of Christ. A great example of *kerygma* is found in First Corinthians 15:3-4, which says, "For I delivered to you first of all that which I also received: that Christ died for our sins according to the Scriptures, and that He was buried, and that He rose again the third day according to the Scriptures" (*NKJV*).

2. *Didache* (Teaching)

This word refers to "doctrine" or "teaching." Once people had responded to the *kerygma* and had put their faith in Christ, it was necessary to teach them and establish them in the truths of the Word of God. After preaching and leading to people to Christ, Paul labored extensively in order to teach them. Referring to Paul's time in Corinth, Acts 18:11 says, "He continued there a year and six months, teaching the word of God among them" (*NKJV*).

3. *Koinonia* (Fellowship)

Part of Thayer's definition for this word is "that in which any person or thing is inherently fixed, implanted, or with which it is intimately connected."[38] Acts 2:42 describes the richness of communion enjoyed by the early Church, saying, "And they continued steadfastly in the apostles' doctrine and fellowship [*koinonia*], in the breaking of bread, and in prayers"(*NKJV*, explanation mine).

4. *Katartismos* (Equipping)

The leaders of the early Church did not see their role as that of *entertaining* the saints, but as that of *equipping* the saints. Ephesians 4:11-12 says, "And His gifts were [varied; He Himself appointed and gave men to us] some to be apostles (special messengers), some prophets (inspired preachers and expounders), some evangelists (preachers of the Gospel, traveling missionaries), some pastors (shepherds of His flock) and teachers. His intention was the perfecting and the full equipping of the saints (His consecrated people), [that they should do] the work of ministering toward building up Christ's body (the church)" (*AMP*). The word, equip (*katartismos*), was used to speak of fishermen repairing their nets, of a doctor setting a bone, or of a house being furnished. It meant to bring something or someone into the condition it was intended to be in so that it was adequate for its intended task.

5. *Diaspora* (Scattering)

Diaspora, which means "scattered abroad," is used twice in Acts chapter 8. Verse 1 says, "At that time a great persecution arose against the church which was at Jerusalem; and they were all scattered throughout the regions

---

[38]Thayer, Greek-English Lexicon of the New Testament (Peabody: Hendrickson Publishers, 1996), 352.

of Judea and Samaria, except the apostles." Verse 4 then says, "Therefore those who were scattered went everywhere preaching the word" (*NKJV*). It's interesting that the first evangelistic scattering of the believers was not in response to prayer or a missions strategy, but it was a reaction to persecution.

6. *Diakonia* (Serving)

You may recognize this word as being somewhat similar to "deacon." It refers to ministry or serving. Jesus not only *modeled* this virtue through His life, but He explicitly said, "The Son of Man did not come to be served, but to serve" (Matthew 20:28, *NKJV*). This reminds us that when we follow the example of the Lord Jesus, we also will seek to serve both the *plan* of God and the *people* of God.

7. *Doxa* (Glory)

Doxa is where we get the word "doxology." The New Bible Dictionary says that this word doxa refers to "the revelation of the character and the presence of God in the Person and work of Jesus Christ. He is the outshining of the divine glory (Heb. 1:3)."[39] Ephesians 3:21 says, "Glory to him in the church and in Christ Jesus through all generations forever and ever! Amen" (*NLT*). It's important for us to remember that we were created for God's glory. In Isaiah 43:7, God says, "Bring all who claim me as their God, for I have made them for my glory" (*NLT*). When we think of giving God glory, we often think of offering Him heartfelt praise and sincere worship. Yes, God is glorified when we praise and worship Him, but Peter indicated that

---

[39]Wood, D.R.W. and I. Howard Marshall. New Bible Dictionary. 3rd Ed. Leicester, England; Downers Grove, IL: InterVarsity Press, 1996.

we also glorify God whenever we serve Him "with the ability which [He] supplies" (1 Peter 4:11, *NKJV*). It should be the aim of every church and every believer to glorify God in everything we do. First Corinthians 10:31 says, "Whatever you do, do it all for the glory of God" (*NLT*).

These seven vital functions and emphases of the early Church can provide a helpful checklist for the local Church. We can study these areas, and then ask ourselves how we're doing in our ministries and churches. Where we sense we're doing well, we can be glad and continue to cooperate with the Lord. If we sense a deficiency in one or more of these areas, we can prayerfully consider how to increase our effectiveness with Heaven's help.

What is it that *you* do well? If your grace pertains most strongly to fellowship and serving, then focus on those with all your heart, but at the same time, appreciate those whose focus is in other areas and allow your strengths to complement theirs. If your grace is in the areas of teaching and preaching, then give yourself to those functions accordingly, but celebrate those whose strengths lie elsewhere. It's when you have all of these areas functioning in a balanced way that you have a healthy church. Don't be prideful because of gifts you have or intimidated because of gifts you lack. Give what you have and cheer on others as they do the same.

A Team Prayer Concerning Authenticity

Father, thank You that we can be who we are. Thank You that we don't have to impress anyone or put on airs. We ask You to protect us from any deceiving influences that would distort the image of who You've created us to be. May our faith and service to You always be genuine and sincere. May our work reflect the apostolic idea of "such as we have, we give." May our service be from our hearts and from what You have done in our lives. May we never slip into hypocrisy in any way, but may we be true to our identity and our calling in You. In Jesus' name we pray, amen

Quotes Worth Remembering

"Sincerity is to speak as we think, to do as we pretend and profess, to perform and make good what we promise, and really to be what we would seem and appear to be."

- John Tillotson

"The first virtue of all really great men is that they are sincere. They eradicate hypocrisy from their hearts."

- Anatole France

"It's the great temptation for small groups of people to slide into a state where they're not quite telling each other the truth and they're not quite celebrating each other. Instead, they tolerate each other, they accommodate each other, and they settle for sitting on the unspoken matters that separate them."[40]

- Bill Hybels

"Nothing is more effective than sincere, accurate praise, and nothing is more lame than a cookie-cutter compliment."

- Bill Walsh

---

[40]Taken from *Axiom: Powerful Leadership Proverbs* by Bill Hybels, Copyright© 2008. Used by permission of Zondervan. www.zondervan.com

"Rabbits don't fly. Eagles don't swim. Ducks look funny try-ing to climb. Squirrels don't have feathers. Stop comparing. There's plenty of room in the forest."

- Charles Swindoll

Questions for Reflection and Discussion

1. Identify someone you know who exhibits authenticity. Describe how you've seen authenticity operate in this person's life and what benefits it produces.

2. Identify a time when you operated in and exhibited authenticity. What were the benefits?

3. Identify a time when you failed to operate in authenticity. Did it create problems? How did you recover?

4. Describe some practical ways that an authentic team functions. What happens when authenticity is part of the team culture?

5. What does a team look like and what happens when authenticity is absent from the team culture?

6. In what ways can you and your team grow in the area of exhibiting authenticity, and how would this bring improvement to the work all of you are doing?

7. Review the five Quotes Worth Remembering. Which of these quotes speaks the most to you and how does it specifically impact you?

Group Exercise: Beyond Authenticity

For the letter "A" in *Champions*, I chose "authenticity." There are other words, though, that begin with the letter "A" that have to do with great teamwork and championship performances. How are you doing and how is your team doing in regard to the following?

Achievers: Are team members striving for high quality results?

Anticipation: Are team members dreaming about and planning for the future?

Attentive: Are team members focusing and paying close attention to their work?

Attitude: Do team members have a good attitude in their work?

Discuss these areas and do some self-assessment with other members of the team. Acknowledge and affirm the areas where the team is doing well. Also discuss how improvement can take place in areas that need it.

CHAPTER SIX

Champions Are Motivated

"Man is made so that whenever anything fires his soul, impossibilities vanish."

- Jean de La Fontaine

One of the best and most beloved sports movies of all times, *Rudy*, is the story of Daniel "Rudy" Ruettiger. As a kid, Rudy always dreamed of playing football for the University of Notre Dame, but monumental hindrances stood in his way. He didn't have the grades or the finances, and he lacked the size, speed, talent, and athleticism to compete at that level. But what Rudy did have was heart. His passion, determination, commitment, resolve, and hustle were unparalleled. In a word, he was motivated.

Rudy was always going full-throttle, giving everything he had—even though he was only on the practice squad—while the naturally gifted players were content to coast, giving 85% in practices. Though Rudy was never a star (he only got to dress for one game and go in at the very end of one game during his college career), he inspired everyone with his tenacity and grit every time he stepped on to the practice field.

Rudy's love for the game caused him to hustle. He simply worked harder than the next guy, pushed himself more, and was determined to maximize the ability he had. He may have been the smallest player on the team, but he had the biggest "want to."

Motivated People Are Passionate

A motivated person is not apathetic, half-hearted, or lackadaisical. He is not flippant, lazy, or casual. Rather, he is sold-out, on-fire, and completely invested with every fiber of his being.

Zechariah 8:2 reads, "This is what the LORD of Heaven's Armies says: My love for Mount Zion is passionate and strong; I am consumed with passion for Jerusalem!" (*NLT*). The word "passion" here refers to *an ardent enthusiasm, a strong emotion or desire*. Dr. Martin Luther King Jr. encapsulated this idea of "passion" when he said, "Even if they try to kill you, you develop the inner conviction that there are some things so precious, some things so eternally true that they are worth dying for. And if a person has not found something to die for, that person isn't fit to live."

Often, our passion for something is what motivates us, and it's what gets us through the hard times. Even when we don't feel like putting forth the required effort, our passion enables us to do what must be done. Hebrews 12:2 says that Jesus "who for the joy that was set before him endured the cross, despising the shame, and has sat down at the right hand of the throne of God" (*NKJV*). What was the joy that was set before Jesus? Was it simply obedience to the Father's will? Was it us? Were we the object of His affection, pursuit, and passion?

Having been created in God's image, we too are called to be a passionate people. Jesus told a scribe who questioned Him, "You must love the

LORD your God with all your heart, all your soul, all your mind, and all your strength." (Mark 12:30, *NLT*). Passion affects everything—our attitude, our perspective, and our actions.

We know when we've lost our passion. It's evident in the way we feel, think, and act. Floyd McClung, a world-wide church planter and leadership trainer, once said, "I know when apostolic passion has died in my heart. It happens when I don't spend my quiet time dreaming of the time when Jesus will be worshiped in languages that aren't yet heard in heaven. I know it's missing from my life when I sing about heaven, but live as if earth is my home. Apostolic passion is dead in my heart when I dream more about sports, toys, places to go and people to see, than I do about the nations worshiping Jesus."[41]

For the Apostle Paul, passion about the Gospel and his heavenly assignment was not a superficial excitement, but a steadfast resolve that manifested itself in rock-solid determination and commitment. Even when great adversity was ahead, Paul was unwavering in his forward momentum.

> *And see, now I go bound in the spirit to Jerusalem, not knowing the things that will happen to me there, except that the Holy Spirit testifies in every city, saying that chains and tribulations await me.*
>
> *But none of these things move me; nor do I count my life dear to myself, so that I may finish my race with joy, and the*

---

[41]Floyd McClung, "Apostolic Passion: What Is Apostolic Passion?", Winds of Renewal, July-September 1999, http://www.missionfrontiers.org/issue/article/apostolic-passion.

> *ministry which I received from the Lord Jesus, to testify to the gospel of the grace of God.*
>
> *Acts 20:22-24, NKJV*

Our goal should be to have the kind of passion that Paul had. We must cultivate and possess the kind of motivation that keeps us going even when struggles and hardships threaten to derail us from the path God has set before us.

Motivated People Hustle

Motivation is that "fire in the belly" that translates into us giving our best for God. It's what people in the sports world call "hustle." A great biblical example of passion and hustle is Titus, one of the helpers who Paul referred to as his "true son" (Titus 1:4).

Paul said of Titus, "But thank God! He has given Titus the same enthusiasm for you that I have. Titus welcomed our request that he visit you again. In fact, he himself was very eager to go and see you" (2 Corinthians 8:16-17, *NLT*). Notice the words "enthusiasm" and "eager." These words reveal Titus' level of passion. The word "enthusiasm" here is the Greek word *spoude*, and is derived from the word for *speed*. My friend, Keith Trump, who is very skilled in the Greek language, states that this word originally meant *haste* or *to hurry up*. It later evolved to take on the connotation of *important*. In other words, what is being communicated when this word is used of Titus is this: 'In light of the importance of the task, Titus was very zealous and diligent in what he did. He was careful and tireless in his task, and he spared no effort in accomplishing it.

Other translations render "enthusiasm" (*spoude*) as:

- the same earnest care (*NKJV*)

- the same devoted concern (*MSG*)

- the same earnest zeal and care (*AMP*)

- dedicated (*GW*)

- eager (*GNB*)

- the same devotion (*NET*)

- the same diligent zeal (*DAR*).

In sports, talent can make a team *good*, but talent plus eager enthusiasm (motivation and hustle) will make a team *great*. The same is true in ministry.

Motivated People Take Initiative

Elbert Hubbard once said, "Parties who want milk should not seat themselves on a stool in the middle of the field and hope that the cow will back up to them." We can take this statement to mean there is always something we can *do*—even if we are patiently waiting for an answer to prayer. Initiative is a big part of motivation and a key to being successful in life and ministry.

I often hear pastors speak appreciatively of people on their team who "get it." These people don't require constant supervision and constant reminders about what needs to be done. They intuitively recognize needs and with wise initiative, address those needs without ever having to be told what to do. This doesn't mean that they are mind-readers or that they don't need training and instruction, but it does mean that they pick up quickly on what needs to be done, and they assume responsibility for getting those things accomplished.

For example, a worker might be told to move boxes of new chairs into a certain classroom. A person who lacks initiative might simply move the boxes into the room and consider the job finished. However, a person with initiative would move the boxes into the room, take the chairs out of the boxes, set the chairs in order, and remove the boxes from the room. If there's any question, the worker will at least say to his or her supervisor, "I assume you want me to set up the chairs and throw away the boxes as well, correct?"

Initiative and thoroughness go hand-in-hand and when these are part of a team's culture, tasks are going to be done—and done well. You won't see a lot of loose ends and things falling through the cracks. Motivated workers stay on top of things and take godly pride in their work.

The Best Motivation Comes from Within

Legendary basketball coach John Wooden said, "There should never be a need for me to give a pep talk to instill motivation. The motivation must come from the player's belief—deeply entrenched—that ultimate success lies in giving their personal best. More than anything, I wanted players to love the process of doing that. Unlike a pep talk that might generate temporary enthusiasm, loving the process of working to be your best isn't temporary. When players truly believe this, giving them a pep talk so they can 'rise to the occasion' is unnecessary; they've already risen to it."[42] I love

---

[42]John Wooden, My Personal Best. (New York: McGraw Hill Education, 2004), 178.

Coach Wooden's quote, but I also believe that he's presenting the ideal. If you are a leader, you can't always assume that your team members are going to be 100% internally motivated. A leader will recognize that his players are at different levels of maturity and self-motivation and will work with them accordingly.

Kevin McHale and Hakeem Olajuwon, two NBA greats, revealed their understanding of self-motivation, saying, "All great players are self motivated,"[43] and "It's not up to anyone else to make me give my best."[44] Former college football coach Lou Holtz said, "Nobody is going to wind you up every morning and give you a pep talk. So be a self-starter."[45] While self-motivation is the ideal goal, a good coach will seek to motivate his team externally while encouraging them and teaching them to develop the skill of self-motivation.

As the Apostle Paul coached and mentored young Timothy, he knew Timothy's tendency toward timidity. Paul encouraged his young protégé to take responsibility for his own spiritual fervor. He told Timothy to "stir up (rekindle the embers of, fan the flame of, and keep burning) the [gracious] gift of God, [the inner fire] that is in you by means of the laying on of my hands... For God did not give us a spirit of timidity (of cowardice, of craven and cringing and fawning fear), but [He has given us a spirit] of power and of love and of calm and well-balanced mind and discipline and self-control" (2 Timothy 1:6-7, *AMP*).

---

[43]Dr. Criswell Freeman, The Book of Basketball Wisdom, Nashville, TN, Walnut Grove Press, 1997, Page 80.
[44]Ibid 122.
[45]Dr. Criswell Freeman, The Book of Football Wisdom, Nashville, TN, Walnut Grove Press, 1996, Page 108.

Be a person who is passionate about the things of God and about what you and your team can accomplish working together. Be a person who hustles and takes initiative. And, finally, be a person who takes responsibility for your own motivation level. Be responsible to stir yourself up and to keep yourself stirred up.

A Team Prayer Concerning Motivation

Father, we determine in our hearts today to be influenced by You, inspired by You, and motivated by You. We believe that serving You is the greatest investment that we could ever make with our lives, and we're thankful that you've given us the privilege and the opportunity to serve You together. May we never take serving You for granted, and may we never do it flippantly or carelessly, but may we serve You with passion, always hustling and giving our best for Your honor and glory. In Jesus' name we pray, amen.

Quotes Worth Remembering

"If you aren't fired with enthusiasm, you will be fired with enthusiasm."[46]

- Vince Lombardi

"A fanatic is one who can't change his mind and won't change the subject."

- Winston Churchill

"Everything comes to him who hustles while he waits."

- Thomas A. Edison

[46]Dr. Criswell Freeman, The Book of Football Wisdom, Nashville, TN, Walnut Grove Press, 1996, Page 113.

"There are no traffic jams on the extra mile."

- Zig Ziglar

"If you travel the earth, you will find it is largely divided into two classes of people—people who say 'I wonder why such and such is not done" and people who say 'Now who is going to prevent me from doing that thing?'"

- Winston Churchill

Questions for Reflection and Discussion

1. Identify someone you know who is highly motivated. Describe how you've seen motivation operate in this person's life and what benefits it produces.

2. Identify a time when you operated in a highly motivated way. What were the benefits?

3. Identify a time when you were not highly motivated. Did it create problems? How did you reestablish motivation?

4. Describe the characteristics of a motivated team and what happens when motivation is part of the team culture.

5. What does a team look like and what happens when motivation is absent from the team culture?

6. In what ways can you and your team grow in the area of being motivated, and how would this bring improvement to the work all of you are doing?

7. Review the five Quotes Worth Remembering. Which of these quotes

speaks the most to you and how does it specifically impact you?

Group Exercise: Beyond Motivation

For the letter "M" in *Champions*, I chose "motivation." There are other words, though, that begin with the letter "M" that have to do with great teamwork and championship performances. How are *you* doing, and how is *your team* doing, in regard to the following?

Maturity: Are team members acting maturely?

Meticulous: Are team members paying attention to important details?

Morale: Are team members contributing to and walking in high morale?

Multiplying: Are team members multiplying their effectiveness through inspiring, recruiting, and training others?

Discuss these areas and do some self-assessment with other members of the team. Acknowledge and affirm the areas where the team is doing well. Also discuss how improvement can take place in needed areas.

CHAPTER SEVEN

Champions Are Persistent

"We know how rough the road will be, how heavy here the road will be, we know about the barricades that wait along the track, but we have set our soul upon a certain goal ahead, and nothing left from hell to sky shall ever turn us back."

- Vince Lombardi

If motivation *gets* you going, persistence will *keep* you going. It's important to understand that passion has to be maintained. It's not enough just to have a burst of excitement and later slough off. Eagerness, enthusiasm, and hustle are all great, but they need to be sustained. We need to be strong finishers as well as eager starters. This is where persistence comes in.

Jessie Owens, winner of four gold medals at the 1936 Berlin Olympics, powerfully expressed the significance of passion that endures. He said, "There is something that can happen to every athlete and every human being; the instinct to slack off, to give in to pain, to give less than your best... the instinct to hope to win through luck or your opponent not doing his best, instead of going to the limit and past your limit, where victory is always to be found. Defeating those negative instincts that are out to defeat us, is the difference between winning and losing, and we face that battle every day of our lives."

Bear Bryant, the famed football coach of Alabama once said, "Don't give up at halftime. Concentrate on winning the second half."[47]

I've seen runners slow down close to the finish line (thinking they had an easy win) only to be passed in the last second of the race by someone who was closing in on them. I've seen football players who flipped the ball behind them right before they crossed the goal line, forfeiting a touchdown. They may have hustled early, but they quit giving their all too soon.

In Super Bowl XXVII, a defensive lineman recovered a fumble and ran it 65 yards for what appeared to be a certain touchdown. He slowed down ten yards before the goal line, and later said he was watching himself on the big screen. He was unaware that a player from the other team was rapidly closing in on him and at the one-yard line, the unprotected ball was slapped out of his outstretched hand, spoiling a touchdown opportunity for him. It's not enough to begin a great play if you quit hustling before you've accomplished your goal.

When Jesus addressed the church at Ephesus, He commended them for many outstanding attributes; they were doing several things well. But then, Jesus confronted them with the following:

> *Nevertheless I have this against you, that you have left your first love.*
>
> *Remember therefore from where you have fallen; repent and do the first works, or else I will come to you quickly and*

---

[47]Dr. Criswell Freeman, The Book of Football Wisdom, Nashville, TN, Walnut Grove Press, 1996, Page 120.

remove your lampstand from its place—unless you repent.

Revelation 2:4-5, NKJV

Later in Revelation, Jesus told the Laodiceans, "Because you are luke-warm, and neither cold nor hot, I will vomit you out of My mouth" (Revelation 3:16, *NKJV*). *The Message* renders that same verse, "You're stale. You're stagnant. You make me want to vomit."

The importance of persistence is made clear in other parts of the Bible. Romans 12:11 says, "Don't burn out; keep yourselves fueled and aflame" (*MSG*). The *Amplified Bible* renders the same verse, "Never lag in zeal and in earnest endeavor; be aglow and burning with the Spirit, serving the Lord." The believers who received the Book of Hebrews had it mixed up: They were letting slip the promises that should have been sticking, and the pressures they should have been letting slide were sticking!

> *Therefore we ought to give the more earnest heed to the things which we have heard, lest at any time we should let them slip.*
>
> *Hebrews 2:1, KJV*

> *But Christ as a Son over His own house, whose house we are if we hold fast the confidence and the rejoicing of the hope firm to the end.*
>
> *Hebrews 3:6, NKJV*

> *For we have become partakers of Christ if we hold the beginning of our confidence steadfast to the end...*
>
> *Hebrews 3:14, NKJV*

> *Therefore do not cast away your confidence, which has great*
> *reward. For you have need of endurance, so that after you*
> *have done the will of God, you may receive the promise...*

> *Hebrews 10:35-36, NKJV*

These believers were becoming Teflon when they should have been Velcro, and vice versa. These verses were written to them to encourage them to be persistent in the promises and will of God and to let everything else go.

Eleazar is an Old Testament figure who was persistent in God's assignment. When God's people were attacked, "Eleazar stood his ground and killed Philistines right and left until he was exhausted—but he never let go of his sword! A big win for GOD that day" (2 Samuel 23:10, *MSG*). The *New King James Version* says that "his hand stuck to the sword." Eleazar refused to quit and exhibited a godly persistence that we would do well to emulate.

Persistence in the Face of Discouragement

Adoniram Judson (1788-1850) is sometimes referred to as the Founder of Modern American Missions. He and his wife, Ann, went to Burma (after being denied entrance to India) when Burma had no known Christians. It was six horrifically difficult years before Judson saw a single decision for Christ, and in his first eleven years, had only twenty converts; yet Judson persevered. He said, "I will not leave Burma until the cross is planted here forever." In spite of a torturous nineteen months in prison, Judson persevered. Judson was so committed to his post that he wrote to England, "Beg the churches to have patience. If a ship were here to carry me to any part of the world, I would not leave my field. Tell the brethren success is as certain as the promise of a faithful God can make it." After 38 years in Burma, Judson had evangelized the nation and translated the Scriptures into the Burmese language. Sometime after his death, a government survey recorded 210,000 Christians in the nation.[48]

Another missionary who demonstrated great persistence was William Carey (1761-1834), who spent seven long years laboring in India before he saw a decision for Christ. He overcame obstacles simply to get to the mission field in the first place. At a ministers' conference, Carey had been told by an older minister, "Young man, sit down. When God pleases to convert the heathen, He will do it without your aid or mine!" Carey was rejected for ordination when he gave his first sermon as a candidate, and did not receive credentials for two additional years.

Carey also understood teamwork. He once said, "I will go down, if you will hold the ropes." Carey and his team translated the Bible into thirty-four Asian languages, produced dictionaries, started schools, churches, and missions stations, and also worked for the rights of women.

William Carey and Adoniram Judson both experienced multiple family tragedies in addition to countless other challenges, and yet their persistence enabled them to keep their hand to the plow. Carey said, "I can plod. I can persevere in any definite pursuit. To this I owe everything." Persistence is more than just not quitting. Persistence means that we not only hang on, but that we also proactively, aggressively, and continually give ourselves to doing God's will with all of the strength and grace He provides.

---

[48]http://www.wholesomewords.org/missions/bjudson1.html

I am sure that well-meaning pragmatists would have encouraged Carey and Judson in their early years on the field "to be reasonable" and to seek more receptive audiences. Yet they persisted in what they believed was God's will for their lives. No doubt these men were influenced by the Apostle Paul, who greatly demonstrated persistence and dedication to the call.

> *And let us not lose heart and grow weary and faint in acting nobly and doing right, for in due time and at the appointed season we shall reap, if we do not loosen and relax our courage and faint.*
>
> *So then, as occasion and opportunity open up to us, let us do good [morally] to all people [not only being useful or profitable to them, but also doing what is for their spiritual good and advantage]. Be mindful to be a blessing, especially to those of the household of faith [those who belong to God's family with you, the believers].*
>
> *Galatians 6:9-10, AMP*

Paul knew there was a tendency (and sometimes even good reason!) to lose heart and grow weary. Still, he encouraged believers to maintain courageous persistence, and he assured us that there is a reward for staying the course.

Persistence in the Face of the Mundane

I've often heard people express frustration because they don't feel their assignment in the Body of Christ is as exciting or as fulfilling as that of others. They may see their work as tedious and monotonous, whereas the work of a missionary or an evangelist seems to be more significant and consequential. It's important to realize, though, that every task in the Body of Christ is significant, and God does not consider anyone's assignment or work unimportant. Jesus said, "If you give even a cup of cold water to one of the least of my followers, you will surely be rewarded" (Matthew 10:42, *NLT*).

One time when David and his men were on a military expedition, the army was given divided assignments. Four hundred of the men continued with David, but two hundred of his men were forced to stay back due to exhaustion. These two hundred weren't idle, however. David tasked them with the responsibility to guard the equipment. After the victory, some of the four hundred soldiers involved in the military action did not want the ones who stayed behind to receive any of the spoils. David protested strongly and declared, "We share and share alike—those who go to battle and those who guard the equipment" (1 Samuel 30:24, *NLT*).

Some people are inclined to think that only the missionary on the front lines is important, but that's not true. If you type letters, keep the books, or clean the carpets, know that what you do is important in the Kingdom of God. Be persistent and consistent in doing your work with excellence. Take heed to Paul's advice to "be strong and immovable. Always work enthusiastically for the Lord, for you know that nothing you do for the Lord is ever useless" (1 Corinthians 15:58, *NLT*).

In another Old Testament story, the enemies of God's people made a serious miscalculation. Having lost a battle against the Israelites, the advisors to the king of Syria said, "Their gods are gods of the hills. Therefore they were stronger than we; but if we fight against them in the plain, surely we will be stronger than they" (1 Kings 20:23, *NKJV*). When Syria was ready to attack God's people using their new strategy, God had a surprise in store for them: "Then a man of God came and spoke to the king of Israel, and said, 'Thus says the Lord: "Because the Syrians have said, 'The Lord is God of the hills, but He is not God of the valleys,' therefore I will deliver all this great multitude into your hand, and you shall know that I am the LORD'"' (1 Kings 20:28, *NKJV*). The Syrians thought that God was geographically limited, that He was restricted in His ability to deliver His people. They thought that Israel's God was only a God of the hills, but God wants us to know that He is the God of the hills, the plains, and the valleys!

How does this apply to us in regard to our being champions for God? Figuratively speaking, the hills represent the high points in our lives, the mountaintop experiences, the times when we feel like we're on top of the world. But God isn't just with us when we're on top of everything. He's also the God of the plains. The plains metaphorically refer to what we consider to be the routine, ordinary, day-to-day aspects of our lives. Richard J. Foster said, "The discovery of God lies in the daily and the ordinary, not in the spectacular and the heroic. If we cannot find God in the routines of home and shop, then we will not find Him at all."[49] God is just as interested in the "plains" in our lives as He is in the hills of our lives! Don't let impatience and a lack of contentment with where you are cause you to think that you're missing it. The grass isn't greener on the other side. What John Burroughs said is typically true: "The lure of the distant and the difficult is deceptive. The great opportunity is where you are."

---

[49] PRAYER: FINDING THE HEART'S TRUE HOME by RICHARD FOSTER. Copyright © 1992 by Richard J. Foster. Reprinted courtesy of HarperCollins Publishers.

I'm thankful that my lungs haven't decided that they're bored because all they do all day long is breathe in and breathe out. That may not seem very exciting to my lungs, but I'm very grateful that they keep doing it. Likewise, there may be some things we do in life that don't seem tremendously exciting, but consistency and persistence are good traits, even if we are persisting in something that seems mundane at times.

Persistence in the Face of Failure

Michael Jordan, considered by many to be the greatest basketball player of all time, said, "I've missed more than 9,000 shots in my career. I've lost almost 300 games. 26 times, I've been trusted to take the game winning shot and missed. I've failed over and over and over again in my life. And that is why I succeed." In reality, our attitude toward failure is always more important than the failure itself. As Henry Ford said, "Failure is simply the opportunity to begin again this time, more intelligently."

The great men of the Bible are not men who never failed, but men who didn't quit. They are not men who never fell, but men who knew how to get up and keep on going. Moses murdered a man. David committed adultery and murdered a man in an attempted cover-up. Peter cut a man's ear off with a sword. Paul persecuted the Church. All of these men failed, all of them needed forgiveness, and all of them needed God's mercy in order to have another chance and a new beginning.

Let me share with you some important things to do when you've experienced failure:

- **Stay hooked up with God:** People seem to have a tendency to resist

God the hardest when they need Him the most.

- **Admit it:** There's something refreshing about just facing up to the facts and admitting that you missed it. Failure in any given situation will do you *more* harm if you refuse to come to grips with what happened. Shifting the blame and choosing to be in denial will only get you into deeper trouble.

- **Be gracious to yourself:** If someone else failed or made a mistake, we would be the first to encourage them. So why do we find it so hard to forgive and encourage ourselves? Be as gracious to yourself as you would be toward others. Forgive yourself. Don't ruthlessly punish yourself.

- **Put it in perspective:** Is it really the end of the world? Is it really that important in the scope of your entire lifetime? Is it really that important in the scope of eternity? Is it worth harboring in your heart and allowing it to affect your future? Will the sun rise in the east tomorrow?

- **Learn from it:** One of the biggest mistakes you can make is to not learn from your mistakes.

- **Forget it:** Don't forget the lessons learned, but don't allow the past failure to be predominant in your thinking or oppressive in your soul. Don't accept past failure as a rule for future living.

- **Regroup:** Reexamine your foundation, goals, methods, timing, and so forth. Make whatever adjustments you need to make.

- **Refuse to give up:** Discouragement is one of Satan's greatest tools in wearing people down. Remember, if you didn't have the potential for success, the enemy wouldn't be fighting so hard to get you to quit. Refuse to wallow in self-pity! Resist the temptation to be discouraged! Refuse to have your vision stolen! You've never really failed until you quit.

- **Don't allow the fear of failure to creep back in:** Some people are paralyzed by the fear of failure. Opportunities are missed and creativity is stifled when people fear failure. Unless you're willing to risk failing, you stand no chance of succeeding.

- **Plan for success:** Let hope and vision be resurrected. Anticipate blessing and favor. Lean on God's strength and wisdom and expect fruitfulness.

Persistence Creates Longevity on the Team

Any seasoned leader will tell you that it's difficult to build a cohesive, efficient team when there is constant turnover among the members. I realize that members will, at times, be directed to another assignment, but there's something healthy for the individual and the church when team members stay put, really grow, and establish tenure and increasing proficiency in their positions. There is a tendency among some to always be hopping from one thing to another—to be in a position just long enough to be able to start prospering and then leave before they have a chance to really make a mark.

If you are a seasoned believer who has been serving God for many years, now is not the time to let up and take it easy. If you have a pulse, you have a purpose. Passionately serve God until you take your final breath. If you are a young believer, purpose in your heart that you will run your race with endurance and that your zeal for serving God will not fade with time.

A Team Prayer Concerning Persistence

Father, You did not create us just to be starters; You designed us to be finishers—and strong finishers at that. We yield our lives to You and ask You to build persistence and endurance into the very core of our being. We pray that we never become lethargic or yield to apathy, but that we will tenaciously pursue Your plan and apply ourselves to Your work until our final breath. May we never grow weary in well doing. Thank You for helping us to never back down in discouragement or cease to value the seemingly small things, and may we never surrender to failure. We embrace Your desire for our lives, which is that we would bear fruit, and that our fruit would remain. In Jesus' name we pray, amen.

Quotes Worth Remembering

"I determined never to stop until I had come to the end and achieved my purpose."

- David Livingstone

"Nothing in this world can take the place of persistence. Talent will not: nothing is more common than unsuccessful men with talent. Genius will not; unrewarded genius is almost a proverb. Education will not: the world is full of educated derelicts. Persistence and determination alone are omnipotent."

- Calvin Coolidge

"Let me tell you the secret that has led me to my goal: my strength lies solely in my tenacity."

- Louis Pasteur

"Never give in. Never, never, never, never- in nothing great or small, large or petty—never give in, except to convictions of honor and good sense."

- Winston Churchill

"Every man is enthusiastic at times. One man has enthusiasm for thirty minutes, another man has it for thirty days, but it is the man who has it for thirty years who makes a success in life."

- Edward B. Butler

Questions for Reflection and Discussion

1. Identify someone you know who is consistently persistent. Describe how you've seen persistence operate in this person's life and what benefits it produces.

2. Identify a time when you exhibited persistence. What were the benefits?

3. Identify a time when you failed to operate in persistence. Did it create problems? What did you do to rectify the situation?

4. What does a persistent team look like and what happens when persistence is part of the team culture?

5. What does a team look like and what happens when persistence is absent from the team culture?

6. In what ways can you and your team grow in the area of exhibiting persistence, and how would this bring improvement to the work all of you are doing?

7. Review the five Quotes Worth Remembering. Which of these quotes speaks the most to you, and how does it specifically impact you?

Group Exercise: Beyond Persistence

For the letter "P" in *Champions*, I chose "persistence." There are other words, though, that begin with the letter "P" that have to do with great teamwork and championship performances. How are you doing and how is your team doing in regard to the following?

Positive: Do you and your team have a positive attitude?

People: How are your people skills? Are you developing and improving these skills and are you working hard to bring out the best in others?

Prayer: Are you maintaining a solid prayer life?

Playful: Are you keeping a good sense of humor and having fun with your fellow team members?

Discuss these areas with other members of the team. Acknowledge and affirm the areas where the team is doing well. Also discuss how improvement can take place in needed areas.

CHAPTER EIGHT

Champions Are Interdependent

"I am a member of a team, and I rely on the team, I defer to it and sacrifice for it, because the team, not the individual, is the ultimate champion."

- Mia Hamm

Interdependence involves mutual reliance in relationships; it is present when members of a group or team are reciprocally dependent upon each other. Interdependence connotes unity, teamwork, cooperation, collaboration, and partnership, and it's an essential trait for any team that is going to be effective.

John Wooden understood and promoted the concept of interdependence (teamwork) perhaps as much as any coach in college basketball history. He said, "The five best players don't necessarily make the best team. Of course, I'd prefer to have my five most talented student-athletes starting a game, but to become a starter, the player needed to combine talent with teamwork. Talent alone would not get you on the starting team."[50] Wooden spoke of how he dealt with one star player—an individual who had more talent than others on the team: "He was too concentrated on having the ball and shooting before he'd look for the pass. This is damaging because among other

---

[50]John Wooden, *My Personal Best* (New York: McGraw-Hill Education, 2004), N 113.

reasons, teammates would soon stop working to get open for a shot, as they know they won't get the ball. It then becomes every man for himself, and the team is destroyed."[51] As a result, Coach Wooden did not allow this "star" to start on the team until he learned how to be a better team player.

Some of the most enjoyable moments in sports happen when there's well synchronized teamwork. Who doesn't love it when a guard is bringing the basketball up the court and dishes a perfectly timed, perfectly placed alley-oop to a teammate for a slam dunk? What about a well-executed tri-ple-play in baseball or a perfectly thrown pass in football to a receiver who's run an excellent route?

In all these cases, team members need to know each other well enough to trust each other. They've practiced enough together to know what each other is capable of and what each person is going to do. The players are committed to each other and willing to be part of a winning equation. They rely on each other and realize that each of them have to fulfill his or her own part for the team to be successful. Whether the basketball player gets the assist, sets an important screen, or makes the basket, each player is a vital part of the process.

Sometimes we see these amazing plays on television, and we forget that all of these finely tuned athletic "machines" were once clumsy little kids who had to develop their balance and coordination. It took years of practice for them to cultivate their individual skills and great diligence to learn how to work smoothly with their fellow team members. They did not start out as elite professionals.

[51]Ibid, 102.

Maybe the team that you're a part of now doesn't perform with the precision of Olympic-caliber synchronized swimmers. Whether it's your marriage, your co-workers at the office, or fellow volunteers or staff members at church, you may not feel like there's a lot of unity and partnership taking place. It's okay to be inspired by a great team, but don't let yourself become discouraged by comparing your team to another. That team you admire had to work through a lot of issues to achieve whatever level of proficiency they've attained. Don't shoot for perfection for your team, but do seek improvement!

Pat Summitt was the coach for the Lady Vols (University of Tennessee women's basketball team) from 1974 to 2012 and led her teams to eight NCAA championships. She made a very realistic assessment when she said, "To me, teamwork is a lot like being part of a family. It comes with obligations, entanglements, headaches, and quarrels. But the rewards are worth the cost." Summitt obviously understood the importance of teamwork, but she also realized that great teamwork doesn't just happen; there are many issues to work through.

Let's think about our teams: What are some of the key indicators that we are not experiencing the kind of interdependence that we need to flourish? I've compiled a list of some of these indicators:

- Not having a "team mentality," meaning there is a determination to look out for one's self ahead of the team—personal (independent) agendas

- Competition instead of collaboration, one-upmanship

- Lack of communication

- Resistance to accountability

- An attitude of entitlement

- Territorialism

- Conflicting or unclear goals

- Discordant values and philosophy

- Disrespect toward authority or other team members

- Cliques and coalitions

- Passive aggressive behavior

- Power plays

- Noncompliance with team guidelines

- Sensitivity and offenses (grudges)

- Talking *about* teammates but not talking *to* teammates

- Lack of trust, suspicion, and paranoia

- Sabotage

- Unrealistic expectations

- Loss of morale

- Disheartened and disillusioned members

- A chill in the air, tension, walking on eggshells

These are some of the things that must be eradicated if we are to have a team in which members operate collaboratively.

Occasionally, a team member fails to make the necessary adjustments to be a positive part of the team. And in some cases, it becomes necessary for a coach to remove a player who is undermining the cohesiveness or effectiveness of the team. Even as I wrote this chapter, it was announced that a professional basketball player was being released indefinitely from his organization for "conduct detrimental to the team." To bring an ancient perspective to this type of situation, Solomon said, "Cast out the scoffer, and contention will leave; Yes, strife and reproach will cease" (Proverbs 22:10, *NKJV*).

On the positive side, many problems can be worked out with patient coaching and instruction. The interdependence and "team chemistry" of Jesus' disciples didn't always function at a healthy level. Jesus had to correct them periodically as they jostled for power and preeminence, but He didn't give up on them.

During Jesus' time on earth, James and John especially struggled to understand the concept of a *team*. We read that "James and John, the sons of Zebedee, came to [Jesus], saying, 'Teacher, we want You to do for us whatever we ask'" (Mark 10:35, *NKJV*). They proceeded to request, "Grant us that we may sit, one on Your right hand and the other on Your left, in Your glory" (Mark 10:37, *NKJV*). Of course, Jesus instructed and corrected them, but then we read, "And when the ten heard it, they began to be greatly displeased with James and John" (Mark 10:41, *NKJV*). All of the disciples were initially dysfunctional when it came to teamwork.

Jesus used occasions like these as teaching moments to convey the importance of servanthood and humility, and it appears the disciples finally got it. The good news is that the disciples who had often argued and contended with one another were "all with one accord in one place" on the Day of Pentecost (Acts 2:1). Their relationships had evolved from chaotic to cooperative, from strife to solidarity.

Consider Paul's teaching on how God designed us for cooperation with one another as interdependent members of the Body of Christ.

> *I want you to think about how all this makes you more significant, not less. A body isn't just a single part blown up into something huge. It's all the different-but-similar parts arranged and functioning together.*
>
> *If Foot said, "I'm not elegant like Hand, embellished with rings; I guess I don't belong to this body," would that make it so?*
>
> *If Ear said, "I'm not beautiful like Eye, limpid and expressive; I don't deserve a place on the head," would you want to remove it from the body?*
>
> *If the body was all eye, how could it hear? If all ear, how could it smell?*
>
> *As it is, we see that God has carefully placed each part of the body right where he wanted it.*
>
> *But I also want you to think about how this keeps your significance from getting blown up into self-importance. For no matter how significant you are, it is only because of what you are a part of. An enormous eye or a gigantic hand wouldn't be a body, but a monster. What we have is one body with many parts, each its proper size and in its proper place. No part is important on its own.*

Can you imagine Eye telling Hand, "Get lost; I don't need you"? Or, Head telling Foot, "You're fired; your job has been phased out"?

As a matter of fact, in practice it works the other way—the "lower" the part, the more basic, and therefore necessary. You can live without an eye, for instance, but not without a stomach.

When it's a part of your own body you are concerned with, it makes no difference whether the part is visible or clothed, higher or lower. You give it dignity and honor just as it is, without comparisons.

If anything, you have more concern for the lower parts than the higher. If you had to choose, wouldn't you prefer good digestion to full-bodied hair?

The way God designed our bodies is a model for understanding our lives together as a church: every part dependent on every other part, the parts we mention and the parts we don't, the parts we see and the parts we don't. If one part hurts, every other part is involved in the hurt, and in the healing. If one part flourishes, every other part enters into the exuberance.

You are Christ's body—that's who you are! You must never forget this. Only as you accept your part of that body does your "part" mean anything.

1 Corinthians 12:14-27, MSG

If we grasp the deep meaning behind Paul's "body" metaphor, we will understand how important each of us are to the other! We need one another, and we are dependent on the work that each of us is called to do.

As stated previously, the Trinity is our model and standard for teamwork. We understand that we are still learning and growing and the perfection of the Father, Son, and Holy Spirit should inspire us, not intimidate us. When we refer to "interdependence" relative to the Trinity, we mean that each member of the Godhead relied completely on the others. It took each member carrying out His respective responsibilities for the work of God to be complete.

The Trinity's Interdependence

Consider, for example, how much Jesus relied upon the Father and the Holy Spirit.

- Jesus did not come of His own initiative but was sent by the Father (John 5:30, 36; 6:57; 7:28-29; 8:16, 18, 29, 42; 12:49; 17:8, 18; 16:28; 17:25).

- Jesus said He could do nothing of Himself but did what He saw the Father do (John 5:19; 5:30; 8:28).

- Jesus did the works of the Father (John 10:32, 37-28) and said it was the Father in Him doing the works (John 14:10).

- Jesus spoke as the Father instructed Him (John 7:16; 8:28, 38; 12:49-50; 14:10; 15:15; 17:8).

- Jesus sought the Father's will (John 5:30) and the Father's glory (John 7:18).

- Jesus said the Father was with Him (John 8:16, 29; 16:32).

- Jesus always did those things that pleased the Father (John 8:29).

- Jesus honored the Father (John 8:49) and was honored by the Father (John 8:54).

- Jesus was known by the Father and knew the Father (John 10:15).

- Jesus said, "I and My Father are one" (John 10:30).

- Jesus said He was in the Father and that the Father was in Him (John 8:38; 14:10-11).

- Jesus said, "He who has seen Me has seen the Father" (John 14:9).

- Jesus said that the Father was glorified in Him (John 14:31).

- Jesus was loved by the Father (John 10:17; 15:9; 17:24) and Jesus loved the Father (John 14:31).

- Jesus kept the Father's commandments and abode in His love (John 15:10).

- Whatever the Father had belonged to Jesus (John 16:15). Jesus said, "All Mine are Yours, and Yours are Mine" (John 17:10).

- Jesus acknowledged that His disciples had been given to Him by the Father (John 17:6, 9, 11-12, 24; 18:9).

- Jesus also taught that our prayer requests were to be addressed to God the Father and made in Jesus' name (John 14:13; 15:16; 16:23).

Teamwork in the Trinity is not restricted to the Father and the Son. Consider the essential contributions and indispensable involvement of the Spirit in Divine Collaboration.

- Jesus was conceived by the Holy Spirit (Matthew 1:20; Luke 1:35).

- John the Baptist said that Jesus would baptize believers with the

Holy Spirit (Luke 3:16).

- Jesus was full of the Spirit (Luke 3:22; 4:1).

- Jesus had the Spirit without measure (John 3:34).

- Jesus was led by the Spirit (Matthew 4:1; Luke 4:1).

- Jesus was anointed by the Spirit (Luke 4:18; Acts 10:38).

- Jesus rejoiced in the Spirit (Luke 10:21).

- Jesus cast out demons by the Spirit (Matthew 12:28).

- Jesus was raised from the dead by the Holy Spirit (Romans 8:11).

- Jesus offered Himself without spot to God through the eternal Spirit (Hebrews 9:41).

- Jesus gave instructions to His disciples by the Spirit (Acts 1:2).

Jesus wanted to make sure that we understand that our relationship with God involves all three members of the Trinity. In John 14:26, Jesus said, "But the Helper, the Holy Spirit, whom the Father will send in My name, He will teach you all things, and bring to your remembrance all things that I said to you" (*NKJV*). Paul said that it's "through [Jesus] we both have access by one Spirit to the Father" (Ephesians 2:18, *NKJV*).

God the Father is for us! God the Son is for us! God the Holy Spirit is for us! We're seeing the seamless, flawless interdependence among the members of the Trinity. And just as Jesus relied completely on the Father and the Holy Spirit, they also relied completely on Him.

Can We Actually "Play" on the Same Side as Team Trinity?

While it might be somewhat easy to recognize the amazing teamwork between the Trinity, it can be harder for us to realize that we have been drafted to play on their team! Sam Storms noted, "God created us so that the joy He has in Himself might be ours. God doesn't simply think about Himself or talk to Himself. He enjoys Himself! He celebrates with infinite and eternal intensity the beauty of who He is as Father, Son, and Holy Spirit. And we've been created to join the party!"[52] What does this mean? Does this mean that we become deity? That we become a fourth member of the Trinity? Hardly. We are human, but we have become "partakers of the divine nature" (2 Peter 1:4, *NKJV*). So, were we created to "join the party?" Absolutely!

We've been called into partnership with God himself. Paul said that "we are labourers together with God" (1 Corinthians 3:9, *KJV*). Mark 16:20 says of the early followers of Jesus, "And they went out and preached everywhere, the Lord working with them and confirming the word through the accompanying signs" (*NKJV*). When we serve God His way, we are interacting with each member of the Trinity.

- Like Jesus, we are under the authority of the Father and are fulfilling His plan. We are emulating Jesus and following His example. Jesus even said, "He who believes in Me, the works that I do he will do also; and greater works than these he will do, because I go to My Father" (John 14:12, *NKJV*). He also said, " As the Father has sent

---

[52]Sam Storms, "A Christian Theory of Everything,", *Sam Storms: Enjoying God,* March 21, 2006 http://samstorms.com/enjoying-god-blog/post/a-christian-theory-of-everything

Me, I also send you" (John 20:21, *NKJV*). Not only do we have the privilege of being born of the Spirit, but we also (like Jesus) have the privilege of being equipped and anointed by the Holy Spirit to do the work of God.

This is a good time to look more closely at what Jesus prayed for us in John 17:21 (*NKJV*) when He prayed "that they all may be one, as You, Father, are in Me, and I in You; that they also may be one in Us, that the world may believe that You sent Me." Notice that Jesus didn't simply pray that we would be one—that we would have some kind of generic unity and teamwork among ourselves. No, He prayed that we would be one *in them*— one with the Trinity! The way *The Message* renders Jesus' words helps shed light on this verse: "The goal is for all of them to become one heart and mind—just as you, Father, are in me and I in you, so they might be one heart and mind with us. Then the world might believe that you, in fact, sent me."

When we serve under the Father's authority, pattern our lives after the Lord Jesus, and operate under the anointing of the Holy Spirit, we essentially become "one heart and one mind" with the Trinity. We become an expression of God, an extension of His love. Paul spoke to the Colossians about "Christ in you, the hope of glory" (1:27, *NKJV*). Paul made that amazing statement to the whole Church. Every believer has been brought into union with God, and we were designed to partner with the Trinity in expressing God's glory in the earth.

Some may have a problem thinking of themselves as a part of "Team Trinity" because of God's flawlessness. Let me share a story that might help make this concept easier to grasp. I am the youngest of four brothers who are six, eight, and ten years older than me. When I was five or six years old, I was not able to compete with them in sports—they were older, bigger, and more developed. But because they were good brothers, they would often let me play with them. They had to be patient because my skills were well below theirs, but the more they allowed me to play with them, the better I became.

In a similar way (but on an even greater scale), we don't measure up to the perfection of the Trinity. However, God graciously allows us to be a part of His team, even though our skills don't measure up to those of the God-head. There is truth, though, to the phrase, "Practice makes perfect." The more we serve, the more our abilities evolve and improve. This is true for us individually and corporately. And God's grace is always there, as is His Word, to build, instruct, correct, and encourage.

In case you're still a bit uncertain about partnering with the Trinity and about being a member (along with the rest of the Body of Christ) of God's Dream Team, you might consider these statements from John's Gospel.

- Jesus said that He is glorified in us (17:10).
- Jesus said He spoke so that His joy might be fulfilled in us (17:13).
- Jesus gave us His Word (17:14).
- Jesus said that we are not of the world, just as He is not of the world (17:14, 16).
- As the Father sent Jesus into the world, so Jesus sent us into the

world (17:18).

- Jesus sanctified Himself so that we could also be sanctified by the truth (17:19).

- Jesus prayed that we would be united in the unity that the Father and the Son share (17:21).

- Jesus gave us the glory that the Father had given Him (17:22).

- Jesus said the love the Father has for Him would be in us (17:26).

Based on how Jesus prayed and how He expressed His heart and desires concerning us, I'd say He has some pretty big plans for us. It sounds like He wants us to realize our union with God and understand that with our sanctification, we've become partakers of His glory and now have a destiny like unto that of Jesus himself.

If Jesus was interdependent with the Father and the Holy Spirit, how much more do we need to be interdependent with God—*and* with the team that we're called to work with, which is to say, others in the Body of Christ? So how are we doing? Have we grown and matured in our teamwork with God and with one another? Let's look at some catalysts and evidences of a team that is flourishing, seasoned, and healthy:

- There is a determination to have great team dynamics. Members don't merely want passive cooperation but they strive for proactive collaboration. Teams with great interdependence intentionally and continually work on it.

- There is a commitment to make each other (and thus the team as a whole) better.

- There is loyalty to one another. Members genuinely care for and pray for one another.

- There is shared commitment to common goals. This includes shared vision, values, and ministry philosophy.

- There is effective communication taking place.

- High standards are expected and maintained.

- Team members have a sense of accountability toward each other; they speak the truth in love to one another.

- Members possess a sense of humor, playfulness, and lightheartedness. Members take the ministry seriously, but they don't take themselves too seriously.

- There is an awareness of each other's shortcomings and the offering of mutual support.

- There is a redemptive history in that team members have been through battles together; they've fought side by side and picked each other up after tough times. They may have even clashed with each other, but they've worked through issues and moved on.

- There is celebration of each other's victories.

- There are realistic expectations. The team shoots for excellence, but avoids setting impossible standards that are disheartening.

- There is respectful diversity. Everyone's unique roles, responsibilities, perspectives, and gifts are respected.

- There is consistency and predictability.

- There is trust with verification.

- The team is resilient. Members are able to bounce back from disappointments and failures.

- There is honesty and vulnerability. Team members are not defensive, touchy, or hiding behind walls. Team members own up to mistakes, receiving correction and instruction that will help them do better in the future.

- There is an awareness of and sensitivity to the needs of others.

Don't let this list intimidate you. With the exception of Team Trinity, every team has room for improvement, and God never starts with perfect people or perfect teams anyway. You may even be frustrated with some of your teammates, but God probably wants you focusing on improving yourself, not on them. Focus on being the best team member you can be and on setting the best example that you can possibly set.

I encourage you to pray for your fellow team members. Let them know how important they are; value them; praise them when they do well; and let them know that you need them. We truly are all in this together.

A Team Prayer Concerning Interdependence

Father, we acknowledge today that we not only rely completely on You, but we are also dependent upon one another. Your Word says that we are the Body of Christ and that individually we are members of one another. Help us to walk in the awareness of how much we need one another and have. In Jesus' name we pray, amen.

Quotes Worth Remembering

"If a team is to reach its potential, each player must be willing to subordinate his personal goals to the good of the team."[53]

- Bud Wilkinson

"Teamwork is what the Green Bay Packers were all about. They didn't do it for individual glory. They did it because they loved one another."

- Vince Lombardi

"The best teams have chemistry. They communicate with each other and they sacrifice personal glory for a common goal."[54]

- Dave DeBusschere

"Some people believe you win with your five best players, but I found out that you win with the five who fit together best."[55]

- Red Auerbach

"I can do things you cannot, you can do things I cannot; together we can do great things."

- Mother Teresa

---

[53]Dr. Criswell Freeman, The Book of Football Wisdom, Nashville, TN, Walnut Grove Press, 1996, Page 71.
[54]Dr. Criswell Freeman, The book of Basketball Wisdom, Nashville, TN, Walnut Grove Press, 1997, Page 72.
[55]Ibid, 63.

Questions for Reflection and Discussion

1. Identify someone you know who exhibits a high level of interdependence. Describe how you've seen this interdependence operate in this person's life and what benefits it has produced.

2. Identify a time when you operated in and exhibited interdependence. What were the benefits?

3. Identify a time when you failed to operate in interdependence. Did it create problems? How did you recover?

4. What does a team look like and what happens when interdependence is part of the team culture?

5. What does a team look like and what happens when interdependence is absent from the team culture?

6. In what ways can you and your team grow in the area of interdependence, and how would this bring improvement to the work all of you are doing?

7. Review the five Quotes Worth Remembering. Which of these quotes speaks the most to you and how does it specifically impact you?

Group Exercise: Beyond Interdependence

For the letter "I" in *Champions*, I chose "interdependence." There are other words, though, that begin with the letter "I" that have to do with great teamwork and championship performances. How are you doing and how is your team doing in regard to the following?

Industrious: Are team members working hard? Is there a good work teamwork and championship performances. How are you doing and how is your team doing in regard to the following?

Industrious: Are team members working hard? Is there a good work ethic?

Innovative: Are team members creative and looking for new and improved ways of doing things?

Indomitable: Are team members incapable of being subdued? Is your team unconquerable?

Intelligence: Are team members working *smart*, and not just working *hard*? Do team members think things through, and is the consideration of facts and knowledge a priority?

Discuss these areas with other members of the team. Acknowledge and affirm the areas where the team is doing well. Also discuss how improvement can take place in areas that need to be strengthened.

CHAPTER NINE

Champions Thrive in Obscurity

"Out of a very intimate acquaintance with D. L. Moody, I wish to testify that he was a far greater prayer than he was preacher."

- R.A. Torrey

Charles Spurgeon and his wife owned chickens, and people noted that they never gave away any of the eggs; they would only sell them. Some people felt they should have been more generous and accused them of being stingy and greedy. The Spurgeons were aware of these rumblings and criticisms, but never responded. It was only after Mrs. Spurgeon passed away that the full story was revealed—the profits from the sale of the eggs were used by the Spurgeons to support two elderly widows. Perhaps their quest for anonymity was based upon their knowledge of what Jesus taught in the Book of Matthew.

Take heed that you do not do your charitable deeds before men, to be seen by them. Otherwise you have no reward from your Father in heaven.

Therefore, when you do a charitable deed, do not sound a trumpet before you as the hypocrites do in the synagogues and in the streets, that they may have glory from men. Assuredly, I say to you, they have their reward.

139

But when you do a charitable deed, do not let your left hand know what your right hand is doing, that your charitable deed may be in secret; and your Father who sees in secret will Himself reward you openly.

Matthew 6:1-4, NKJV

Jesus went on to convey the same sentiments regarding prayer in verses 5-8 and concerning fasting in verses 16-18.

The point Jesus is making is not that it's wrong to be seen doing something for God; some positions require some visibility. You can't go to your pastor and say, "Pastor, I'd like to be a greeter at church, but I don't want anyone to see me." There's no such thing as an invisible greeter. It's not wrong if someone sees you serving God, but it's wrong if being seen is your motivation. If you're only serving God for the recognition and applause of others in order to meet an ego-need in your own life, that's a problem.

Church work is much like an iceberg; the bulk of it is out of sight, invisible to the casual observer. When many people think of church, they think about what they see, hear, and experience during the Sunday morning service. While those aspects are important, they're only a fraction of what church is really about. It's important to remember all the planning, prayer, and preparation that happen behind the scenes. It's important to remember the relationships of the people and the care, communication, and support that are exchanged as individuals interact throughout the week. Just because something is not highly visible does not mean that it lacks value and significance.

Our emphasis should always be on substance, not on image. Paul warned about "those who pride themselves on surface appearances [on the virtues they only appear to have], although their heart is devoid of them" (2 Corinthians 5:12, *AMP*). It's been noted that reputation is what people *think* we are, but character is what we *really* are. If we'll take care of and focus on our character—the inward qualities of our lives—we'll have no problems with our reputation.

We may be extremely surprised when we get to Heaven and see how God actually rewards people. There may be some whose work was highly visible, who actually receive little-to-no rewards because they operated with wrong motives. There may be others whose work was unknown to and unseen by others, who will receive great rewards.

Aspects of Jesus' ministry were highly visible. In John 18:20 He said, "I spoke openly to the world. I always taught in synagogues and in the temple...and in secret I have said nothing" (*NKJV*). And yet, just as an iceberg's larger mass is below the surface—unseen to the passing sailor—much of Jesus' greatness was birthed in obscurity.

Jesus' years in submission to His parents and at the carpenter's bench far exceeded His time in public ministry. We know that Jesus operated before men in great wisdom and power, but He also cultivated a profound prayer life in solitude. Luke 6:12 says, "It came to pass in those days that [Jesus] went out to the mountain to pray, and continued all night in prayer to God" (*NKJV*).

Franklin Delano Roosevelt once said that what he wanted on his staff were young men with a passion for anonymity. Oliver Wendell Holmes stated, "The best servant does his work unseen." Effective servants of God are not simply good in public, but they excel behind the scenes—they thrive in obscurity.

The word "obscure" means:

- Shrouded in or hidden by darkness

- Not clearly seen or easily distinguished

- Not readily understood or clearly expressed

- Relatively unknown

- Not prominent or famous

Do you only work hard when the boss is watching? Do you only "act" spiritual when you're at church? God doesn't want our Christianity to be a show that we put on at certain times; He wants us to be genuine, real, and sincere. This means that we aspire unto godliness, holiness, and Christlikeness regardless of whether or not anyone is watching.

I recently taught at a conference for pastors and church staff on the topic of thriving in obscurity, and one staff member in his twenties mentioned to me afterward that this is a very important message for the younger generation to hear. Many feel compelled to take a "selfie" and post it to social media regardless of whether they're driving the car, drinking coffee, or simply eating. There seems to be a quest to be noticed, and while this need to be seen is part of human nature and modern culture, our assignment is not to promote ourselves, but to make Christ known.

In sports, athletes know they can't just flip a switch and step into peak-performance at game time if they haven't been training and practicing diligently behind the scenes. The test of a true champion is not found in the desire to excel while others are watching, but rather in the dedication to be disciplined and diligent when no one is watching. Legendary boxer Joe Frazier, said, "You can map out a fight plan or a life plan, but when the action starts,… you're down to your reflexes… That's where your roadwork shows. If you cheated on that in the dark of the morning, you're going to get found out now, under the bright lights." In short, it's what you do in private that helps you become a success in public.

A Divine Helper

The Holy Spirit is One who thrives in obscurity. He works hand-in-hand with the Father and the Son, and yet He does much of His work behind the scenes—softly, discreetly, and subtly. He is pleased to exalt and draw attention to the Father and to Jesus. Though He made a dramatic entrance on the Day of Pentecost (Acts 2:1-4), we more often sense His still small voice (1 Kings 19:12) and His affirming witness within (Romans 8:16). Rather than drawing great attention to Himself, the Holy Spirit delights in fulfilling His role and His assignment, which Jesus clearly articulated:

> *However, when He, the Spirit of truth, has come, He will guide you into all truth; for He will not speak on His own authority, but whatever He hears He will speak; and He will tell you things to come.*
>
> *He will glorify Me, for He will take of what is Mine and declare it to you.*

All things that the Father has are Mine. Therefore I said that He will take of Mine and declare it to you.

John 16:13-15, NKJV

The Holy Spirit facilitates the work of God in our hearts. He glorifies Jesus, and He administers that which Jesus and the Father have for us. In referring to the Holy Spirit, Jesus calls Him, "another Helper."

And I will pray the Father, and He will give you another Helper, that He may abide with you forever—the Spirit of truth...

John 14:16-17, NKJV

One commentary says that usage of the word Helper (*Paraclete*) "denotes 'one called in,' or 'called to the side of another,' for the purpose of helping him in any way."[56]

Jesus' usage of the word "another" in reference to the Holy Spirit implies two things. First, the disciples had already known a Helper. And, second, that initial Helper was Jesus himself (1 John 2:1). The Greek word for "another" implies that the Holy Spirit is *similar in nature* or *another of like kind* to the first Helper, Jesus. The Holy Spirit does not have a separate agenda or a nature contrary to the nature of Jesus.

Here's what we know. Jesus called the Holy Spirit *another* Comforter. This means that the Holy Spirit is similar in nature to Jesus himself and has been called alongside us to help us. It has been taught, and rightly so, that many believers have been assigned by God to serve in what is often called

---

[56]H. D. M. Spence-Jones,ed. The Pulpit Commentary St. John Vol. II, (London; New York: Funk & Wagnalls Company, 1909), 226.

the ministry of helps (1 Corinthians 12:28). Those who serve in "helps" often serve behind the scenes; they are unsung and often unnoticed heroes in the Body of Christ. But the ultimate "Helps Minister" is the Holy Spirit himself.

While Jesus ministered upon the earth, the Father and the Holy Spirit were essentially unseen, and yet the Father's plan was made visible through Jesus. And the Holy Spirit's empowerment fueled and made possible all that Jesus did. Thank God for what Jesus did visibly, but thank God as well for all that the Holy Spirit has done and continues to do invisibly—or behind the scenes.

Are you content with being unseen? Are you willing to function as a human *paraclete* the same way the Holy Spirit functions as a divine *Paraclete*? Are you willing to work behind the scenes and not draw attention to yourself? Are you willing to help someone else be successful and facilitate the work of God in the lives of others? Are you willing to be called alongside others to help them in any way necessary?

John the Baptist had been highly visible and was actually the center of attention at one point. He did not fight to maintain his prominence, however. Instead, he gladly deferred to Jesus saying, "He must increase, but I must decrease" (John 3:30, *NKJV*). In sharp contrast to John the Baptist's humility is the narcissistic, ladder-climbing, popularity-seeking Diotrophes, spoken of in Third John 9. The Apostle John says that Diotrophes "likes to put himself first" (*ESV*) and that he "loves to have the preeminence" (*NKJV*). In Kingdom work, the point is not about who gets noticed, but rather to ensure that the work is done well. A person who is willing to thrive in obscurity is one who is willing to focus on small things, the details to which no one else pays attention. Some things may seem insignificant, but they are not.

For a natural example of how even the smallest, seemingly insignificant things are vitally important, consider this adaptation of an old poem.

For lack of a nail, the horseshoe was lost.

For lack of a horseshoe, the horse was lost.

For lack of a horse, the rider was lost.

For lack of a rider, the message was lost.

For lack of a message, the battle was lost.

For lack of a battle, the war was lost.

And all for the lack of care about a horseshoe nail.

This little poem illustrates the value of the often unnoticed and unappreciated tasks in life. We may applaud the noble rider who delivers the message, but without the skilled and careful work of a farrier, the rider might never arrive.

People who work behind the scenes provide tremendously valuable service to the Body of Christ, and their willingness to thrive in obscurity is evidence of solid spiritual maturity. In describing the God kind of love, which should be working in all of us, Paul said that it is not "vainglorious" and "does not display itself haughtily" (1 Corinthians 13:4, *AMP*). Another translation says that love "does not parade itself" (*NKJV*). Teams are blessed when players care more about getting the job done than whether or not they get noticed doing the job.

A Team Prayer Concerning Obscurity

Father, thank You for helping each of us to thrive in obscurity and to have the spiritual depth to not care whether we are noticed or recognized for what we do. We know that if we serve You with all of our hearts without regard to the praise or attention of men, we will receive an eternal reward from You that can never be taken away. Help us to stay focused on substance more than image, and to work on our character, not merely our reputation. Help us to pay attention to the important details of life and ministry and to be good human paracletes—ones called alongside to help—just as the Holy Spirit is the divine Paraclete. Help us to work diligently without caring who gets the credit and without drawing attention to ourselves. In Jesus' name we pray, amen.

Quotes Worth Remembering

"Our time of training in secret must far exceed our time of acting in public."

- C.H. Mackintosh

"If you have skills, it's easy to play the game. But it's what you do off the field that dictates whether or not you're a star."[57]

- Willie Mays

"The vision of a champion is bent over, drenched in sweat, at the point of exhaustion, when nobody else is looking."

---

[57]Dr. Criswell Freeman, The Wisdom of Old Time Baseball, Nashville, TN, Walnut Grove Press, 1996, Page 74.

- Mia Hamm

"Quality means doing it right when no one is looking."

- Henry Ford

"Spectacular achievement is always preceded by unspectacular preparation."

- Robert H. Schuller

Questions for Reflection and Discussion

1. Identify someone you know who thrives in obscurity. Describe how you've seen this trait operate in this person's life and what benefits it produces.

2. Identify a time when you did well thriving in obscurity. What were the benefits?

3. Identify a time when you did not thrive in obscurity. Did it create problems? What did you do to rectify the situation?

4. What does a team thriving in obscurity look like, and what happens when thriving in obscurity is part of the team culture?

5. What does a team look like and what happens when thriving in obscurity is absent from the team culture?

6. In what ways can you and your team grow in the area of thriving in obscurity, and how would this bring improvement to the work all of you are doing?

7. Review the five Quotes Worth Remembering. Which of these quotes speaks the most to you, and how does it specifically impact you?

Group Exercise: Beyond Obscurity

For the letter "O" in *Champions*, I chose "obscurity." There are other words, though, that begin with the letter "O" that have to do with great teamwork and championship performances. How are you doing and how is your team doing in regard to the following?

Observant: Are team members alert and watching to know what is going on? Do they pay attention to important details?

Optimistic: Is there a hopeful attitude and a positive atmosphere among team members?

Organized: Are things done decently and in order? Is there good communication among team members? Are things planned thoroughly?

Opinions: Are team members free to share their thoughts, perspectives, and opinions? Are team members able to be mature when their opinions are not shared by others or reflected in the course that is established?

Discuss these areas with other members of the team. Acknowledge and affirm the areas where the team is doing well. Also discuss how improvement can take place in weaker areas.

CHAPTER TEN

Champions Aspire to Nobility

"And the glory which You gave Me I have given them, that they may be one just as We are one."

John 17:22, NKJV

Athletes of noble character seek to honor the sport in which they participate; they believe the sport is bigger than they are. They desire to dignify the game and not disgrace it in any way. Because they respect the sport and those who have played before them, they give their best effort and seek to elevate the game in the eyes of others, and to encourage excellence in those who will follow in their footsteps.

The 1968 Olympic decathlon champion Bill Toomey reflected this kind of attitude when he said, "When I competed, it was for honor and country. It was a privilege to be a part of the U.S. team."

When we believe that life is sacred and that it is a privilege to have been given the gift of life, we will be grateful and seek to honor our Creator.

Perhaps John Wooden's excellence in coaching was due, at least in part, to the fact that his father taught him to make each day his masterpiece. When it comes to serving God in the ministry, these principles are especially true. Being called to ministry is an honor and privilege, and it should bring forth the best that is within us.

Speaking of the priesthood, or being called to ministry, Hebrews 5:4 says, "No one elects himself to this honored position. He's called to it by God, as Aaron was" (*MSG*). It's important to remember that we—all of us in the Body of Christ—are "a chosen generation, a royal priesthood, a holy nation, His own special people, that you may proclaim the praises of Him who called you out of darkness into His marvelous light" (1 Peter 2:9, *NKJV*). Paul told Timothy that God "has saved us and called us with a holy calling" (2 Timothy 1:9, *NKJV*). In the same epistle, Paul said, "In a great house there are not only vessels of gold and silver, but also of wood and clay, some for honor and some for dishonor. Therefore if anyone cleanses himself from the latter, he will be a vessel for honor, sanctified and useful for the Master, prepared for every good work" (2 Timothy 2:20-21, *NKJV*). Scripture teaches that Christ gave Himself for the Church "that He might present her to Himself a glorious church, not having spot or wrinkle or any such thing, but that she should be holy and without blemish" (Ephesians 5:27, *NKJV*). Peter said that God has "called us to His own glory and excellence" (2 Peter 1:3, *ESV*).

It is a glorious privilege and honor to serve God, whether our assignment seems prestigious or not. David said, "A single day in your courts is better than a thousand anywhere else! I would rather be a gatekeeper in the house of my God than live the good life in the homes of the wicked" (Psalm 84:10, *NLT*). We need to remember that dignity and nobility are not established by the seeming prestige of the work we do, but by the magnificence and grandeur of the One for whom we work. Charles Spurgeon said, "If

God calls you to be a minister, don't stoop to become a king."

Those who aspire to nobility in their work for God realize that their example matters. Just as we can "make the teaching about God our Savior attractive in every way" (Titus 2:10, *NLT*), we can also bring reproach to the Gospel and tarnish the cause of Christ by exhibiting an ungodly attitude or engaging in ungodly behavior. Paul was mindful of our roles as ambassadors for Christ (2 Corinthians 5:20, *NKJV*) and expressed a great desire to avoid doing anything that would hinder the gospel of Christ (1 Corinthians 9:12, *NKJV*). In other words, we work for glorious King Jesus, and we want to represent Him well!

If we truly believe that God is in what we do, then we will esteem our work and invest our best into it. Kenneth Hagin wrote, "Fill your place with dignity. If you are called of God to stand in an office, that office demands respect. If you have respect for the office you are in, you will teach people to have respect for that office."[58] If we fail to value our assignment, we may disdain our work and be easily sidetracked. However, if we truly esteem the work of God, it will be much easier to fulfill Paul's admonition to "be steadfast, immovable, always abounding in the work of the Lord, knowing that [our] labor is not in vain in the Lord" (1 Corinthians 15:58, *NKJV*).

Nehemiah exhibited this steadfast, immovable position as he sought to complete his assignment in Jerusalem. Enemies badgered and harassed him, but he refused to lose focus. They appealed time and again for him to come and meet with them, but he responded repeatedly, "I am doing a great work,

---

[58]Kenneth E. Hagin, *The Ministry Gifts*, (Tulsa, OK: Faith Library Publications, 1998), 23.

so that I cannot come down. Why should the work cease while I leave it and go down to you?" (Nehemiah 6:3, *NKJV*).

Jesus was committed to magnifying the Father, and His determination was evidenced in His simple statement, "I have glorified You on the earth. I have finished the work which You have given Me to do" (John 17:4, *NKJV*). Jesus not only glorified His Father by *finishing* the work, but Jesus also glorified the Father by doing all of the work *with excellence*. Mark 7:37 says, "And they were overwhelmingly astonished, saying, He has done everything excellently (commendably and nobly)!" (*AMP*). This verse applies specifically to the miracles and healings Jesus ministered, but I believe Jesus carried out all of His activities here on earth with excellence and nobility, because He was mindful that His whole earthly life was meant to bring glory to God.

What are some of the traits that we see when people truly aspire to nobility?

People Who Aspire to Nobility Appreciate Their Heritage

It's important for us to remember that the Gospel did not start with us. Others have gone before us, paid an immeasurable price, and made enormous sacrifices so that we could hear and read the Word of God and worship freely. Jesus told His disciples, "Others have labored, and you have entered into their labors" (John 4:38, *NKJV*).

If we're not careful, we can take many things for granted. The next time you hold your Bible, remember the men and women who risked death—and the many who actually died—so that we could read the Word of God in our own language. Thank God for the martyrs and others of faith who loved Truth more than mere mortal existence. Their lives, their faith, and in many cases, their deaths, challenge us to respect and honor a most godly heritage.

We often read Hebrews 12:1 without its preceding context. Here's how it reads, though, with the two previous verses included. These verses refer to the patriarchs of old.

> *All these people earned a good reputation because of their faith, yet none of them received all that God had promised.*
>
> *For God had something better in mind for us, so that they would not reach perfection without us.*
>
> *Therefore, since we are surrounded by such a huge crowd of witnesses to the life of faith, let us strip off every weight that slows us down, especially the sin that so easily trips us up. And let us run with endurance the race God has set before us.*
>
> *Hebrews 11:39-40; 12:1, NLT*

Are we running our race with endurance? Are we running the race in way that brings glory to God, earning a good reputation because of our faith?

Acts 13:36 says that David "served God's will and purpose and counsel in his own generation" (*AMP*). We must do the same in our generation. We have a heritage that has been left for us, and we must take up the banner of faith in our generation as our forefathers did in theirs. Billy Graham conveyed this same idea when he said, "I am only one in a glorious chain of men and women God has raised up through the centuries to build Christ's church and take the Gospel everywhere."

People Who Aspire to Nobility Value the Significance of Their Current Work

You need to believe that your work for God is vital and important. It may not be glamorous in the eyes of men, but the advancement of the Kingdom is a noble cause and every effort toward that end is important. A big ego is not helpful to anyone, but a strong conviction about the significance of working for God certainly is. I think that's why Paul said, "I lay great stress on my ministry and magnify my office" (Romans 11:13, *AMP*).

I've had the privilege of visiting several of the beautiful cathedrals in Europe and one of my favorites is St. Paul's Cathedral in London. After St. Paul's was destroyed by fire in 1666, Sir Christopher Wren, one of the great architects of all time, was commissioned to rebuild the cathedral.

During the rebuilding process, Wren (who was unknown to many of the laborers) was surveying the reconstruction and asked some of the workers what they were doing. The first responded that he was cutting some stone. The second responded that he was earning a certain wage. But the third responded, "I am helping Sir Christopher Wren build a beautiful cathedral for the glory of God!"

Perspective is everything. If you're working for God, you're not just going through the motions or taking up space. You're not just cleaning a building, running sound, driving a bus, or working with kids. You are helping Jesus build His Church! He deserves our best and our highest; He deserves our everything! This is why Paul instructed, "Whatever you do or say, do it as a representative of the Lord Jesus, giving thanks through him to God the Father" (Colossians 3:17, *NLT*).

People Who Aspire to Nobility Seek to Leave a Positive Legacy

In the movie *Gladiator*, Maximus was right when he told his men, "What we do in life echoes in eternity."[59] The idea of legacy does not connote a narcissistic attempt to make a name for one's self; it is not an ego-based goal. Rather, legacy is a by-product of a life poured out for the benefit of others and for the glory of God. Spiritually speaking, legacy is not a monument erected to exalt one person, but it's a deposit made that equips other people for greater service.

Having understood this principle, we also understand that when we serve God with humility and excellence, He bestows favor upon us. Jesus said, "If anyone serves Me, him My Father will honor" (John 12:26, *NKJV*). We see the idea of legacy in both the Old and New Testaments, and we understand that legacy involves both this life and the life to come because of the connection between the gift and the giver. Consider these Scriptures:

> *We have happy memories of the godly, but the name of a wicked person rots away.*
>
> *Proverbs 10:7, NLT*

> *...the good deeds of some people are obvious. And the good deeds done in secret will someday come to light.*
>
> *1 Timothy 5:25, NLT*

> *And I heard a voice from heaven saying, "Write this down:*

---

[59]*Gladiator*, Dir. Ridley Scott. Dream Works Distribution, 2000. Film.

Blessed are those who die in the Lord from now on. Yes, says the Spirit, they are blessed indeed, for they will rest from their hard work; for their good deeds follow them!"

Revelation 14:13, NLT

The Bible shows the importance of leaving a godly legacy. Not only will we be rewarded for our good deeds (on earth and in Heaven), but others will also reap the benefit of our having lived a life unto the Lord.

Dorcas is a great example of a person who left a rich legacy. Scripture says of her, "She was always doing kind things for others and helping the poor" (Acts 9:36, *NLT*). We read that after her death, the room where people had gathered " was filled with widows who were weeping and showing him the coats and other clothes Dorcas had made for them" (Acts 9:39, *NLT*). Dorcas left a legacy of kindness and generosity, and we should aspire to do the same.

This reminds me of what Calvin Coolidge said: "No person was ever honored for what he received. Honor has been the reward for what he gave." May we be known as givers, not takers, and may we leave every person we've ever encountered richer for having known us.

A Team Prayer Concerning Nobility

Father, may we always be mindful that we are a royal priesthood, that You have called us with a holy calling, and that You have called us to be vessels unto honor. Like Nehemiah, we believe that we are doing a great work because it is work You have assigned, and it is for Your praise that we do it. Like Jesus, may we do everything excellently, commendably, and nobly. You have given us Your glory, and we recognize the sacredness of the privilege we have in serving You and Your people. We ask that You help us do so with honor and nobility. In Jesus' name we pray, amen.

Quotes Worth Remembering

"Whatever you are, be a good one."

- Abraham Lincoln

"If you be faithful, you will have that honor that comes from God: his Spirit will say in your hearts, Well done, good and faithful servants."

- Adam Clarke

"Quality is never an accident. It is always the result of intelligent effort."

- John Ruskin

"I long to accomplish a great and noble task, but it is my chief duty to accomplish small tasks as if they were great and noble."

- Helen Keller

"If you want to achieve excellence, you can get there today. As of this second, quit doing less-than-excellent work."

- Thomas J. Watson

Questions for Reflection and Discussion

1. Identify someone you know who aspires to nobility. Describe how you've seen nobility operate in this person's life and what benefits

it produces.

2. Identify a time when you operated in and exhibited a sense of nobility. What were the benefits?

3. Identify a time when you failed to operate in nobility. Did it create problems? What did you do to rectify the situation?

4. What does a team look like and what happens when aspiring to nobility is part of the team culture?

5. What does a team look like and what happens when a sense of nobility is absent from the team culture?

6. In what ways can you and your team grow in aspiring to nobility and how would this bring improvement to the work all of you are doing?

7. Review the five Quotes Worth Remembering. Which of these quotes speaks the most to you and how does it specifically impact you?

Group Exercise: Beyond Nobility

For the letter "N" in *Champions*, I chose "nobility." There are other words, though, that begin with the letter "N" that have to do with great teamwork and championship performances. How are you doing and how is your team doing in regard to the following?

Nurture: Do team members encourage one another? Are relationships life-giving and healing in nature?

Navigation: Are team members good at working through problems and going in the right direction?

Natural: Do team members focus on excellence in natural things as much as spiritual things?

Nourish: Do team members nourish themselves? In addition to giving out, do they take time to take in and receive?

Discuss these areas with other members of the team. Acknowledge and affirm the areas where the team is doing well. Also discuss how improvement can take place in needed areas.

CHAPTER ELEVEN

Champions Are Strategic

"An intelligent plan is the first step to success. The man who plans knows where he is going, knows what progress he is making and has a pretty good idea of when he will arrive. Planning is the open road to your destination. If you don't know where you are going, how can you expect to get there?"

- Basil S. Walsh

There came a time during my high school years when I had to make a decision about sports. I had played basketball through my junior year, but I knew it was questionable if I would make the team my senior year. I had started playing tennis as a sophomore, and I was starting to excel more in that sport than in basketball. At the beginning of basketball tryouts my senior year, I told the coach, "I realize I'm on the bubble as far as making the team goes. If you don't think I can make a solid contribution to the team, please go ahead and cut me so I can focus on tennis this winter." Ultimately, I did not make the basketball team that year, so I poured myself into a winter tennis league at a local club. That focus enabled me to raise my skill level and helped me later when I played tennis for Butler University.

As disappointed as I may have been at the time, I believe the coach's decision to cut me from the basketball team was the best choice for both the basketball team as a whole and for me as an individual athlete. The coach made a strategic decision that I respected. A big part of success is having the right people on the team and then having those people in the right positions. For my basketball coach, he had to consider that year's team, and he also had to consider giving underclassmen experience so he could build for the future. Personally, I found it more helpful to focus my energies on one sport (tennis) so I could excel at a higher level in that sport rather than to keep trying to compete in multiple sports.

In churches, sometimes there are people who have been faithful, yet they lack the talent or skill to perform the quality of work that needs to be done. Often, though, workers continue to give sub-par performances that actually hinder the team because the leadership doesn't want to hurt the feelings of a person who has been faithful for many years.

Maybe we as workers should be willing to go to the pastor and say, "I've served in this capacity for a long time and I enjoy doing it. However, if you ever have someone who can do a better job than me and help the team more than I can, please let me know and I'll gladly serve in another area where I can be more beneficial to the church."

We never want to disrespect people's faithful service or fail to appreciate their labor of love, but we also need to be strategic and place people in positions where they can be most effective and productive.

The dictionary defines "strategy" as *a careful plan or method for achieving a particular goal usually over a long period of time.*[60] As I ponder this

---

[60]Merriam-Webster Dictionary, s.v. "strategy."

definition, it seems to me that God is the ultimate strategic planner. Some people seem to feel that if something is truly spiritual, it must be unplanned and spontaneous. However, a consideration of various biblical examples reveals that many godly people have operated strategically.

- When we look at God's work in creation, it's apparent that He was functioning as a Master Strategist. There were distinct stages and orderly phases of God's creative process.

- Proverbs 21:5 tells us, "The plans of the diligent lead surely to plenty..." (*NKJV*). Proverbs 24:6 says, "Strategic planning is the key to warfare; to win, you need a lot of good counsel" (*MSG*).

- Moses had great spiritual revelation from God, and yet he lacked some technical "know how" when it came to administration and management. Fortunately, he was humble enough to listen to advice from his father-in-law; Jethro taught Moses how to be wise and strategic in his leadership (Exodus 18:13-26). Moses learned about defining his own role and responsibilities, identifying and selecting qualified assistants, delegating specific responsibilities, and creating an effective organizational structure.

- God said to His people in captivity, "For I know the plans I have for you,… They are plans for good and not for disaster, to give you a future and a hope" (Jeremiah 29:11, *NLT*).

- Paul's ministry was conducted very strategically. Jesus said Paul's ministry would be focused on "Gentiles, kings, and the children of Israel" (Acts 9:15, *NKJV*). As Paul traveled, his strategy was typically to preach Christ in the synagogues until he was no longer welcome there. His initial converts were often Jewish, and then, using that core group as a base, he would begin reaching out to the Gentiles in that city. As a church got established, Paul would continue to nurture the believers there (often through his representatives, such as Timothy or Titus, and/or through his epistles). Eventually, local leadership would be appointed according to qualifications he communicated in First Timothy 3:1-13 and Titus 1:5-9. Paul would also typically go to larger population centers and establish a work there. Outlying areas would be reached as a result (Acts 19:8-10).

• Ephesians 1:11 says that we have been "predestined according to the purpose of Him who works all things according to the counsel of His will" (*NKJV*). In Ephesians 3:11, we read that what God is doing in and through the Church is in accordance with "the eternal purpose which He accomplished in Christ Jesus our Lord" (*NKJV*).

• In teaching a local church about the healthy operation of spiritual gifts, Paul said, that God "is not a God of confusion and disorder but of peace and order." Later Paul says that "all things should be done with regard to decency and propriety and in an orderly fashion" (1 Corinthians 14:33, 40, *AMP*).

Strategy in itself is not a bad thing. Some people may strategize for selfish purposes, and this motivation turns strategy into a kind of manipulation. But in and of itself, a strategy is simply a careful plan designed to achieve a goal. The Bible is full of examples of God's people being strategic. The important thing is have godly goals!

Nehemiah as a Great Strategist

Nehemiah was God's man to lead the project of rebuilding the walls and gates of Jerusalem following Israel's Babylonian captivity. Having served under the Persian King Artaxerxes, Nehemiah was undoubtedly familiar with leadership principles, organizational structure, and management skills. Often, as in the case of Nehemiah, God will use a person's executive, administrative, or business background for Kingdom work. At other times, God chooses and uses people who seemingly have no background whatsoever that qualifies them for the task at hand (e.g., Gideon in Judges 6:15).

Consider some of the following observations made about Nehemiah:

Tyndale's Commentary says, "As the king's 'cup-bearer' (Nehemiah 1:11), he held a position of great responsibility and influence in the Persian court. Not only did he drink first of the king's wine to guard against poisoning, but he also kept accounts and exercised other administrative responsibilities. Only a person of exceptional trustworthiness would be given such a post."[61]

Another commentary says, "This officer, in the ancient Oriental courts, was always a person of rank and importance; and, from the confidential nature of his duties and his frequent access to the royal presence, he possessed great influence."[62]

Warren Wiersbe described the transition that would have taken place

---

[61]Robert B. Hughes and J. Carl Laney, *Tyndale Concise Bible Commentary*, The Tyndale reference library (Wheaton, IL: Tyndale House Publishers, 2001). 175.
[62]Robert Jamieson, A. R. Fausset and David Brown, *Commentary Critical and Explanatory on the Whole Bible* (Oak Harbor, WA: Logos Research Systems, Inc., 1997). Neh. 1:11.

when Nehemiah left the king's service and embarked on the mission of rebuilding a devastated city:

"The king's cupbearer would have to sacrifice the comfort and security of the palace for the rigors and dangers of life in a ruined city. Luxury would be replaced by ruins, and prestige by ridicule and slander. Instead of sharing the king's bounties, Nehemiah would personally pay for the upkeep of scores of people who would eat at his table. He would leave behind the ease of the palace and take up the toils of encouraging a beaten people and finishing an almost impossible task. And with the help of God, he did it! In fifty-two days, the walls were rebuilt, the gates were restored, and the people were rejoicing! And it all started with a man who cared."[63]

Let's do a walk-through of the process that was involved with Nehemiah's leadership. It was not only divinely favored, but it was also full of strategic thought and action.

1. Before strategy came into play, there was a great, passionate stirring in Nehemiah's heart. After hearing of the great distress of Jerusalem, Nehemiah "sat down and wept, and mourned for many days; [he] was fasting and praying before the God of heaven" (Nehemiah 1:4, *NKJV*).

2. Nehemiah then "networks." He presents his cause to the king and receives permission to go to Jerusalem and rebuild it. Nehemiah also sets a time for this to happen. In addition, he receives letters of authorization from the king and petitions the king for the necessary

---

[63]Warren W. Wiersbe, *Be Determined, "Be" Commentary Series* (Wheaton, IL: Victor Books, 1996). 21-22.

resources (Nehemiah 2:1-9). He's laying preparatory groundwork for the project.

3. Nehemiah does a complete overview of the project—a personal inspection of the damage to the city walls, assessing the work that needs to be done (Nehemiah 2:12-16).

4. Nehemiah gives hope to the people, casting vision for a better future that is to be experienced as they carry out the plan of rebuilding. He gives the task credibility by telling them about God's support and the king's backing (Nehemiah 2:17-18).

5. Work begins to be done by many people. The people take responsibility for repairing different sections of the wall and gates. Everybody has a part to play (Nehemiah 3:1-32).

6. As a leader, Nehemiah has to address both internal and external conflicts among the people.

• Internally, the people are weary (Nehemiah 4:10). There is also conflict among the people, as the rich oppress the poor through the practice of usury (charging excessively high interest on loans). Nehemiah addresses and resolves these issues.

• Externally, there are threats throughout the rebuilding process. Nehemiah refuses to be distracted or diverted from the work by threats and deception from his enemies. Opposition is noted and dealt with different ways:

   • **Nehemiah 2:10:** The opposition is noted. No response is necessary or given.

- **Nehemiah 2:19-20:** The opposition is expressed and met with a firm reply.

- **Nehemiah 4:1-23:** The opposition intensifies and specific threats are made. Nehemiah responds by seeking God and praying. Also, pre-emptive and defensive measures are taken to prepare for a possible attack. A security watch is created; workers are armed; encouragement is given; and a communication system and response plan are established.

- **Nehemiah 6:1-14:** Nehemiah discerns conspiracy and deception and avoids the treachery.

7. After the wall was rebuilt, a number of organizational and managerial processes come into place.

- A city manager is appointed (Nehemiah 7:1-3).

- A census is established (Nehemiah 7:4-73).

- The Word of God is declared and explained. The people are deeply moved; they rejoice, repent, and consecrate themselves to God (Nehemiah 8-10).

- Nehemiah institutes reforms (Nehemiah 13:1-31).

No Bible-believing person doubts that God ordained and blessed the rebuilding of Jerusalem walls, and yet we see that strategic planning and processes were used throughout the rebuilding endeavor. Such methodical approaches would help us be more efficient and productive in accomplishing our goals as well.

Jesus: Spiritual and Strategic

Jesus was not only spiritual; He was also strategic in the way He thought and operated. Consider the strategic components that accompanied the supernatural multiplication of the loaves and fishes.

When the day began to wear away, the twelve came and said to Him, "Send the multitude away, that they may go into the surrounding towns and country, and lodge and get provisions; for we are in a deserted place here."

But He said to them, "You give them something to eat." And they said, "We have no more than five loaves and two fish, unless we go and buy food for all these people."

For there were about five thousand men.

Then He said to His disciples, "Make them sit down in groups of fifty."

And they did so, and made them all sit down.

Then He took the five loaves and the two fish, and looking up to heaven, He blessed and broke them, and gave them to the disciples to set before the multitude.

So they all ate and were filled, and twelve baskets of the leftover fragments were taken up by them.

Luke 9:12-17, NKJV

What do we learn from this story? First, the disciples saw the need, but they saw no way to meet it (they said, "Send the multitude away..."). Second, Jesus challenged the disciples' faith by asking them to do something they could not possibly do in their own physical strength or natural ability.

Third, supernatural miracles and natural organization are friends, not enemies. We often think of the supernatural component of this story—Jesus miraculously multiplying the loaves and fish. However, there are natural, strategic elements to this story as well:

- Organization: Jesus had the disciples seat the people in groups of fifty.

- Delegation: Jesus had the disciples distribute the food to the groups.

- Efficiency: Twelve baskets of the leftover fragments were gathered up.

The spiritual and the practical are complimentary, not contradictory. Strategy benefits our natural lives, but it even has its place in the spiritual lives of believers.

When Jesus talks about the cost of discipleship, He uses a natural illustration that deals with strategic planning.

> *"But don't begin until you count the cost. For who would begin construction of a building without first calculating the cost to see if there is enough money to finish it?*
>
> *Otherwise, you might complete only the foundation before running out of money, and then everyone would laugh at you.*
>
> *They would say, 'There's the person who started that building and couldn't afford to finish it!'*
>
> *"Or what king would go to war against another king without first sitting down with his counselors to discuss whether his army of 10,000 could defeat the 20,000 soldiers marching*

against him?

And if he can't, he will send a delegation to discuss terms of peace while the enemy is still far away.

Luke 14:28-32, NLT

We often hear it preached that we must "count the cost," but do we realize that counting the cost is a strategic principle that requires forethought and careful planning with goals in mind?

Throughout His ministry and leadership, Jesus demonstrated skillful strategy:

- Jesus operated with a keen sense of timing. He regularly referenced timing ("The time is fulfilled," "My time has not yet come," "My time is at hand," "The hour has come...").

- Jesus selected and trained disciples; He gave them hands-on training in the form of various assignments, and He provided mentoring and feedback.

- Jesus clearly articulated His values and defined the mission that His followers were to undertake.

Jesus wanted His disciples to operate strategically, too. Before He ascended, He told them, "You shall receive power when the Holy Spirit has come upon you; and you shall be witnesses to Me in Jerusalem, and in all Judea and Samaria, and to the end of the earth" (Acts 1:8, *NKJV*). Notice there is a strategic progression in this: First, the disciples were to receive power from the Holy Spirit. Jesus had told them not to depart Jerusalem until the Holy Spirit came and filled them with power from heaven (Luke

24:49). Then, they were to witness in Jerusalem (Acts 1-7), then in Judea and Samaria (Acts 8:1-9:31), and then to the ends of the earth (Acts 9:32-28:31). Jerusalem was their home base. Judea was their "state," or the region in which Jerusalem was located. Samaria was the neighboring state with which the Jews had a long-standing strained relationship (*see* Luke 9:51-56 and John 4:9). "The ends of the earth" referred to the Gentile world well beyond the boundaries of Israel. God's compassion sent Jesus to the earth and the disciples to the harvest, but strategy was involved in both commissions.

Strategy and Smoke Detectors

Over the years, I have seen people who are committed to praying for revival, and that is good. I've seen others who are frequently prophesying that there is a great move of God coming soon, and I'm certainly excited about anything God desires to do in the earth. However, anticipation doesn't take the place of action.

Prayer is vital and prophesying is wonderful! Great things are born in the Spirit. But if people don't take action—and, hopefully, *strategic action*—we may never see results or needed changes taking place. Frederick Douglas once said, "I prayed for twenty years but received no answer until I prayed with my legs." Too often we pray and wait, expecting God to do something, while He's actually waiting for *us* to act! And we'll do so more effectively if we have a strategy.

John Carter is a friend who pastors a great church in Syracuse, New York. While he was teaching through the Book of James verse by verse, he was convicted by the Holy Spirit for the church to start being intentionally focused on meeting the needs of the poor in the church and in the community. He sensed the Spirit saying to him, "Pray, and I'll show you the needs to meet." Shortly afterward, John noticed a series of news reports where young children had died in house fires. In each of these sad occasions, there was no smoke detector in the house where the fire occurred. John sensed the Holy Spirit saying, "I want you to do something about this."

John and members of his team discovered that the houses where children had died were in low-income areas of the city. Realizing that smoke detectors could have saved lives, John set out to make a difference and "Operation Firestop" was born. A strategy was necessary to implement the plan conceived in compassion and prayer, and the same God who birthed this idea in Pastor John also gave him wisdom for an effective way to make the dream a reality. Here's how the strategy unfolded:

- Church leaders met with members of the local fire department and established a working relationship with them.

- The vision was shared with the congregation, volunteers were solicited, and funds were raised for the project.

- Church representatives went to a home improvement store and presented the project to them. The store extended a 50% discount on 5,000 smoke detectors, which the church purchased with funds collected from the congregation. The congregation also purchased the batteries needed for the initial installation.

- Using maps of Syracuse, routes were drawn to show the areas of the city most likely in greatest need.

- Approximately 120 church members volunteered and were divided into teams of three. A member of the fire department accompanied each team, and the teams canvassed the targeted areas loaded with ladders, new smoke detectors, and batteries.

- As they knocked on doors, the teams let people know that in response to the recent fire-related tragedies in the community, Abundant Life Church and the Syracuse Fire Department were providing and installing smoke detectors free of charge and providing fire safety instruction.

- Six months later, church members went back to the homes with new batteries (also purchased by the congregation), showed people how to change the batteries, and left the family an extra set of batteries. This gave church teams another opportunity to share the love of God.

As a result of "Operation Firestop," thousands of lives were touched. The number of deaths by fire went down in the area, and many people began a relationship with Jesus because of the care and compassion of the church. The church now sets aside ten percent of its finances for foreign and home missions, and the members continue to strategically reach out to their community.

I believe that all churches can plan and function strategically, and individual believers can utilize strategy in their own lives as well. This kind of purposeful planning in order to reach considered and meaningful goals is another part of being a champion and a fruitful member of a successful team.

A Team Prayer Concerning Strategy

Father, we believe that You are the Master Strategist, and because we are created in Your image, we know that You do not want us to be chaotic, erratic, or haphazard in our work for You. We ask You to give us wisdom, and we pray that You will inspire our hearts and minds so that we will think Your thoughts after You. Thank You for helping us to be orderly, organized, thorough, and strategic in all that we do. We ask that our plans would be plans that You have inspired, and we trust You for guidance and direction as we carry out these plans for Your glory and for the benefit of others. In Jesus' name we pray, amen.

Quotes Worth Remembering

"The loftier the building, the deeper the foundation must be."

- Thomas a Kempis

"If you fail to plan, you are planning to fail!"

- Benjamin Franklin

"A good plan is like a road map: it shows the final destination and usually the best way to get there."

- H. Stanley Judd

"Make no little plans; they have no magic to stir men's blood."

- Daniel Burnham

"The secret of getting ahead is getting started. The secret of

getting started is breaking your complex overwhelming tasks into small manageable tasks, and then starting on the first one."

- Mark Twain

Questions for Reflection and Discussion

1. Identify someone you know who is strategic. Describe how you've seen having a sense of strategy operate in this person's life and what benefits it produces.

2. Identify a time when you operated strategically. What were the benefits?

3. Identify a time when you failed to operate strategically. Did it create problems? How did you recover?

4. What does a team look like and what happens when a strategic mindset is part of the team culture?

5. What does a team look like and what happens when a strategic mindset is absent from the team culture?

6. In what ways can you and your team grow in operating strategically and how would this bring improvement to the work all of you are doing?

7. Review the five Quotes Worth Remembering. Which of these quotes speaks the most to you and how does it specifically impact you?

Group Exercise: Beyond Strategic

For the letter "S" in *Champions*, I chose "strategic." There are other words, though, that begin with the letter "S" that have to do with great team-work and championship performances. How are you doing and how is your team doing in regard to the following?

Stability: Do team members operate in personal stability and bring stability to the rest of the team?

Standards: Do team members maintain appropriate expectations for themselves? Do they work toward healthy goals and ideals?

Skilled: Do team members exhibit skillfulness in their work? Is there a commitment to each one growing in their respective skills?

Significance: Do team members see the value in what they do? Do they delight in adding value to others?

Discuss these areas with other members of the team. Acknowledge and affirm the areas where the team is doing well. Also discuss how improvement can take place in areas that need attention.

CHAPTER TWELVE

The 12th Man

"If you want to go fast, go alone. If you want to go far, go together."

- African Proverb

If you are a football fan, you've most likely heard of "the 12th Man." The term has been used differently at various times, but in recent years it has been used to describe the extremely enthusiastic fans of the National Football League's Seattle Seahawks. A football team is only allowed to have eleven players on the field at a time, but the Seattle fans have the reputation of cheering so voraciously that it gives their team an advantage akin to having an extra player on the field. Many teams in many sports have enthusiastic fans, but the 12th Man in Seattle pride themselves on being the loudest and most boisterous fans of all.

I was in Seattle preaching the weekend after the Seahawks won the NFC title in January 2014, and here's some of what I discovered during that visit.

• Throughout the city, I saw fans wearing jerseys bearing the number 12. I also saw flags and banners with the number 12. I learned that a massive flag with the number 12 on it has been raised at every home game since 2003.

• According to the team's website, the fans cheered so loudly on one touchdown run in 2011 that it actually caused a small earthquake.[64]

- In December 2013, a Guinness world record was established when the 12th Man registered a decibel reading of 137.6 in a game against the New Orleans Saints. That's louder than the noise of a jet taking off from 100 meters away, and just a few decibels lower than the noise on an aircraft carrier flight deck.[65]

When a team has fans cheering for them like that, it gives them a definite edge, a distinct advantage. Visiting teams do not like playing in Seattle. Opponents receive more off-side penalties because they can't hear the count, and opposing quarterbacks are thwarted in calling audibles because the rest of their team can't hear what they are saying at the line of scrimmage.

When we speak of the 12th Man, we're talking about fans who have an influence on how their team plays. Because of the fans, the team's performance is enhanced, and they are inspired to play their very best. In short, the fans make the team better! The 12th Man may not be on the actual field of battle, so to speak, but they aren't disengaged or passive. The 12th Man makes a significant contribution to the team and helps them to victory!

The concept of an influential 12th Man applies in many areas. It was said that when Napoleon was on the battlefield with his men, his army fought so much more valiantly that it was like the French had an additional 40,000 soldiers on the field. Think of it! All because Napoleon was with them!

What should we learn from this? Whether it's a multitude or an individual, the 12th Man can inspire others to perform better, giving them wings

[64]http://www.seahawks.com/12-Man/
[65]Ibid.

to soar! Every one of us needs encouragement and inspiration. Not only do we need a 12th Man to cheer for us, but we also need to be a 12th Man for others. We need to be cheering others on and encouraging them as they run their race.

Who is our 12th Man and who is cheering us on in our journey? What is it that inspires us and bolsters our performance?

1. God and the angels of Heaven are our 12th Man.

Consider these two Scriptures.

> *There will be more joy in heaven over one sinner who repents than over ninety-nine just persons who need no repentance....*
>
> *There is joy in the presence of the angels of God over one sinner who repents.*
>
> *Luke 15:7,10, NKJV*

> *The Lord your God in your midst, The Mighty One, will save; He will rejoice over you with gladness, He will quiet you with His love, He will rejoice over you with singing.*
>
> *Zephaniah 3:17, NKJV*

We need to know that when we gave our lives to Jesus and received His gift of forgiveness and eternal life, there was a celebration in Heaven. Angels rejoiced over us. We see from Zephaniah that God not only loves us, but He also celebrates us! The Bible says He rejoices over us and sings over us. We may not be able to hear God rejoicing over us, but we can accept by faith that God is the 12th Man cheering us on!

After describing our homeward journey toward Heaven, Max Lucado described what our arrival might be like: "You'll see the faces that are waiting for you. You'll hear your name spoken by those who love you. And, maybe, just maybe—in the back, behind the crowds—the One who would rather die than live without you will remove his pierced hands from his heavenly robe and . . . applaud."[66] Does it sound shocking to you that Jesus might possibly applaud us?

Remember the scripture that says when Jesus comes, He will "bring to light the hidden things of darkness and reveal the counsels of the hearts. Then each one's praise will come from God" (1 Corinthians 4:5, *NKJV*). Every believer should yearn to serve the Lord in such a way that we will ultimately hear Him say, "Well done, thou good and faithful servant" (Matthew 25:21, *KJV*). I realize that's speaking of a future reward, but I believe we can, by faith, walk with a sense of God's approval even now and with our spiritual imagination, perceive Him cheering us on as we continue in our journey.

2. The Saints of old—those who have already run their race and are now seated in the grandstands of Heaven—are cheering us on. They are also our 12th Man.

Hebrews chapter 11 records many of the great "heroes of faith." By faith Abel, Enoch, Noah, Abraham, Sarah, Moses, and so many others, believed God and did great exploits. As soon as this chapter concludes, the very next verse (Hebrews 12:1) says, "Therefore we also, since we are surrounded by

---

[66]Used by permission. The Applause of Heaven, Max Lucado, 1994, Thomas Nelson. Nashville, Tennessee. All rights reserved.

so great a cloud of witnesses..." (*NKJV*).

> *Do you see what this means—all these pioneers who blazed the way, all these veterans cheering us on? It means we'd better get on with it. Strip down, start running—and never quit! No extra spiritual fat, no parasitic sins.*
>
> *Keep your eyes on Jesus, who both began and finished this race we're in. Study how he did it. Because he never lost sight of where he was headed—that exhilarating finish in and with God—he could put up with anything along the way: cross, shame, whatever. And now he's there, in the place of honor, right alongside God.*
>
> *Hebrews 12:1-2, MSG*

The idea is that all these heroes of faith have now taken their seats in the grandstands of Heaven and are cheering us on as we run *our* race. They're our 12th Man!

3. As brothers and sisters in Christ, we are to be a 12th Man to one another.

Paul had some people in his corner—he had a 12th Man when he really needed one!

> *Then Jews from Antioch and Iconium came there; and having persuaded the multitudes, they stoned Paul and dragged him out of the city, supposing him to be dead.*
>
> *However, when the disciples gathered around him, he rose up and went into the city. And the next day he departed with Barnabas to Derbe.*
>
> *Acts 14:19-20, NKJV*

Other translations say, "The disciples formed a circle around him" (*ISV*), and "The disciples surrounded him" (*HCSB*). This is why fellowship with other believers is so important. If you ever get beat up, knocked down, and knocked out like that, who is going to gather around you, form a circle around you, and surround you? And, an equally important question—are you ready to be part of a team that surrounds, supports, and prays for someone else who's been knocked down?

In another situation, Paul had been through a terrible storm (Acts 27). The ship he'd been sailing on was destroyed, and he had to swim to shore. On shore, it was cold and wet, and a snake bit him. From a circumstantial standpoint, it was a miserable season in Paul's life. When he was finally making his way toward Rome in chains, he met fellow believers who encouraged him. Acts 28 says, "And so we came to Rome. The believers in Rome heard about us, and came as far as the towns of Market of Appius and Three Inns to meet us. When Paul saw them, he thanked God and was greatly encouraged" (14-15, *GNB*). These believers who came out to greet Paul were truly a 12th Man to him! These believers had probably traveled somewhere between 33 and 43 miles on foot just to show their love, appreciation, and respect to Paul, and it touched him deeply. Paul ministered to and encouraged many. No doubt he was a 12th Man to countless people, but there were also times when he needed a 12th Man himself. We all need the Body of Christ!

Hebrews 10:24-25 gives us clear directions: "Let's see how inventive we can be in encouraging love and helping out, not avoiding worshiping together as some do but spurring each other on, especially as we see the big

Day approaching" (*MSG*). William Barclay said, "One of the highest of human duties is the duty of encouragement.... It is easy to laugh at men's ideals, to pour cold water on their enthusiasm, to discourage them. The world is full of discouragers; we have a Christian duty to encourage one another. Many a time a word of praise or thanks or appreciation or cheer has kept a man on his feet. Blessed is the man who speaks such a word."[67] Let's make the idea of the 12th Man a part of our culture and prevailing atmosphere in our churches. Let's have our fellowships be places where those who are running their races are regularly encouraged, lifted, and celebrated.

What actions make you a member of the 12th Man? What does "cheering loudly for the team" look like in practical application?

- When you love and encourage others, you are a 12th Man!

- When you pray for others, for your church, and for the leadership, you are a 12th Man!

- When you tithe and give generously, you are a 12th Man!

- When you serve faithfully and enthusiastically, you are a 12th Man!

Not everyone can be the star quarterback, but everyone in the Body of Christ can contribute significantly to the team, and encouraging others as a 12th man is a vital contribution.

Remember that Jesus' prayer is that our unity and teamwork be like that of the Trinity. As we allow God to work in our lives and as we apply ourselves to the championship traits we've addressed, we can and will be God's

---

[67]William Barclay, *The Letter to the Hebrews, The Daily Study Bible Series*, (Philadelphia, PA: The Westminster John Knox Press, 1975).

Dream Team in the earth. And, like Paul, we can finish our course with joy, and celebrate our victories together.

Quotes Worth Remembering

"The really great man is the man who makes every man feel great."

- G.K. Chesterton

"Do not keep the alabaster boxes of your love and tenderness sealed up until your friends are dead. Fill their lives with sweetness. Speak approving, cheering words while their ears can hear them and while their hearts can be thrilled and made happier by them."

- Henry Ward Beecher

"If I had my life to live over, I would spend more time encouraging others."

- F.B. Meyer

"There are high spots in all of our lives and most of them have come about through encouragement from someone else. I don't care how great, how famous or successful a man or woman may be, each hungers for applause."

- George M. Adams

"You throw batting practice, you warm up pitchers, you sit and cheer. You do whatever you have to do to stay on the team."

- Bob Uecker

Questions for Reflection and Discussion

1. Identify someone you know who is a great encourager. Describe how you've seen the gift of encouraging others operate in this person's life and what benefits it produces.

2. Identify a time when you operated as an encourager—as a 12th Man. What happened?

3. Identify a time when you missed an opportunity to be an encourager. How did you resolve not to miss such opportunities in the future?

4. What does a team look like and what happens when a 12th Man mindset is part of the team culture?

5. What does a team look like and what happens when a 12th Man mindset is absent from the team culture?

6. In what ways can you and your team grow in being a 12th Man, and how would this bring improvement to the work all of you are doing?

7. Review the five Quotes Worth Remembering. Which of these quotes speaks the most to you and how does it specifically impact you?

ADDENDUM

Understanding the Trinity through Church History

"What good is it for you to be able to discuss the Trinity with great profundity, if you lack humility, and thereby offend the Trinity?"

- Thomas a Kempis

Larry Crabb related the story of an unpleasant experience that happened when he was in the ninth grade. For years, he'd had difficulty with stuttering and often found himself embarrassed, especially in public settings. In one church service, he prayed over the communion elements, and it didn't go well. He writes:

Filled less with worship than with nervousness, I found my theology becoming confused to the point of heresy. I remember thanking the Father for hanging on the cross and praising Christ for triumphantly bringing the Spirit from the grave. Stuttering throughout, I finally thought of the word 'Amen' (perhaps the first evidence of the Spirit's leading), said it, and sat down.[68]

How can we not feel his pain? His "heresy" was obviously inadvertent and unintentional, but he felt angst over it nonetheless.

---

[68]Taken from *Encouragement : The Unexpected Power of Building Others Up* by Dr. Larry Crabb, Copyright © 1990, 1996, 1999. Used by permission of Zondervan. www.zondervan.com

As I wrote this book, I found myself repeatedly wanting to make sure that I would not present any wrong ideas about the Trinity. I have a reverential fear of God, and I do not want to misrepresent Him (or mislead others about Him) in any way.

There is an element of mystery to the Trinity that transcends the comprehension of our finite minds. It seems we strive in vain to find words, metaphors, or analogies to help convey the amazing truth of the Trinity. It is inevitable that our feeble attempts will fall short of completely describing an infinite, eternal God. The Bible says:

> *To whom then will you liken God? Or what likeness will you compare to Him?*
>
> *Isaiah 40:18, NLT*

> *To whom will you liken Me, and make Me equal and compare Me, that we should be alike?*
>
> *Isaiah 46:5, NKJV*

Nevertheless, people have tried to explain what defies complete understanding. Of the metaphors that have been used to try to illustrate the Trinity, some are more helpful than others, but none are perfect.

Some of these metaphors include:

- The three-leafed clover, as explained by St. Patrick

- Water: It takes on three forms—liquid, vapor, and solid.

- A triangle: It is one object with three sides.

- An egg: Again, it is one object, but it's comprised of yolk, white, and shell.

- Space, which can be spoken of in terms of length, width, and depth.

- An apple: This is one fruit but it has a peel, meat, and core.

- Sun, heat, and light

- Multiplication (1 x 1 x 1 = 1)

- Music (a three-note chord)

Some of these are limitedly helpful—they get us thinking about unity and plurality. However, no analogy can ever convey the majesty and grandeur of God. Pressed too far, an illustration can give the idea that there are three gods instead of One God who exists in three persons, or at the other extreme, that the Godhead involves just one person who takes on three roles.

For example, a common attempt to explain the Trinity goes something like this: "I am a man, but I stand in different roles in life: husband, father, and minister." The problem with this illustration is that it conveys the idea that God is one person who simply takes on three different modes at different times. Hence, this error is called "modalism," and it significantly misrepresents the Trinity—the One God who exists eternally in three persons.

While I don't feel the "teamwork" analogy—that there is one team with different players—is misleading (I wouldn't use it if I felt it was), I acknowledge that it has its limitations in describing the Trinity. As a result, I want to share some important expressions of faith from throughout Church history to make sure that readers have a good overview of how the Trinity has been presented through centuries past.

I was raised in a mainline denominational church, and the Trinity was ever before us. We sang the Doxology every Sunday as the service ended. I sang it so many times I've never forgotten the words:

> *"Praise God from Whom all blessings flow.*
>
> *Praise Him all creatures here below.*
>
> *Praise Him above ye heavenly host.*
>
> *Praise Father, Son, and Holy Ghost."*

I must admit that until somewhere in my teenage years I thought the second line stated, "Praise Him, all preachers here below." At some point, I finally realized that this song was not an admonition just for preachers, but for all of God's creation.

We also regularly sang the "Gloria Patri." Its words are, "Glory be to the Father, and to the Son, and to the Holy Ghost. As it was in the beginning, both now and ever shall be, world without end, Amen, Amen." We also periodically sang a beautiful hymn which included the line, "Holy, holy, holy! Merciful and mighty! God in three persons, blessed Trinity."

Another historic piece that strengthened and reinforced my belief in the Trinity was the Apostles' Creed. I don't recall us reciting it every single Sunday, but we made this confession of faith more often than not.

The Apostles' Creed

Though not written by the original twelve apostles, this ancient Church creed reflects and summarizes well the beliefs held dear by the early Church.

I believe in God the Father Almighty,

Maker of heaven and earth;

And in Jesus Christ

His only Son our Lord,

Who was conceived by the Holy Spirit,

born of the Virgin Mary,

suffered under Pontius Pilate,

was crucified, dead, and buried;

He descended into hell;

the third day He arose again from the dead;

He ascended into heaven,

and sits at the right hand of God the Father Almighty;

from thence He shall come to judge the living and the dead.

I believe in the Holy Spirit;

the holy catholic Church;[69]

the communion of saints;

the forgiveness of sins;

the resurrection of the body,

and the life everlasting.

The Nicene Creed

The Creed of Nicea was originally composed in 325 A.D. in response

---

[69]The word "catholic" does not refer to the Roman Catholic Church but to the Universal Church—the entire Body of Christ as a whole.

to controversies concerning the person of Christ and the Trinity. Of major concern was the heretical teaching of Arius, who claimed that Jesus was a created being, thus inferior to God. The Nicene Creed states the following:

"We believe in one God, the Father, the Almighty, maker of heaven and earth, of all that is, seen and unseen.

We believe in one Lord, Jesus Christ, the only Son of God, eternally begotten of the Father, God from God, Light from Light, true God from true God, begotten, not made, of one Being with the Father;

Through him all things were made. For us and for our salvation he came down from heaven, was incarnate of the Holy Spirit and the Virgin Mary, and became truly human. For our sake he was crucified under Pontius Pilate; he suffered death and was buried.

On the third day he rose again in accordance with the Scriptures; he ascended into heaven and is seated at the right hand of the Father. He will come again in glory to judge the living and the dead, and his kingdom will have no end.

We believe in the Holy Spirit, the Lord, the giver of life, who proceeds from the Father [and the Son], who with the Father and the Son is worshiped and glorified, who has spoken through the prophets.

We believe in one holy catholic[70] and apostolic Church. We acknowledge one baptism for the forgiveness of sins. We look for the resurrection of the dead, and the life of the world to come. Amen."

---

[70]The word "catholic" does not refer to the Roman Catholic Church, but rather, the Universal Church - the entire Body of Christ as a whole.

Well before the Council of Nicea, one of the early Church fathers named Irenaeus spoke clearly of the Father, Son, and Holy Spirit. Born around 130 A.D., Irenaeus had been taught by Polycarp of Smyrna, who had been a disciple of the Apostle John. Irenaeus said, "We believe in one God the Father Almighty, 'who made heaven and earth and the sea and all that is in them' (Exodus 20:11); and in one Christ Jesus, the Son of God who became incarnate for our salvation; and in the Holy Spirit, who through the prophets predicted the plan of God."[71]

Throughout Church history, other councils have resulted in creeds—such as the Athanasian Creed, the Chalcedonian Creed, and the Westminster Confession—that articulate and reinforce the nature and significance of the Trinity, namely, that God is one in essence and three in person. In more modern times, Evangelical and Pentecostal groups have also expressed biblically based views regarding the Godhead.

Dallas Theological Seminary, for example, includes the following statement about the Godhead in their Doctrinal Statement: "We believe that the Godhead eternally exists in three persons—the Father, the Son, and the Holy Spirit—and that these three are one God, having precisely the same nature, attributes, and perfections, and worthy of precisely the same homage, confidence, and obedience."[72]

The Assemblies of God Statement of Fundamental Truths also speaks to the issue of identity and cooperation in the Godhead: "The Father, the Son

---

[71]Bryan M. Litfin, Getting to Know the Church Fathers. Brazos Press, Grand Rapids, MI. 2007. Page 95.
[72]http://www.dts.edu/about/doctrinalstatement/

and the Holy Spirit are never identical as to Person; nor confused as to relation; nor divided in respect to the Godhead; nor opposed as to cooperation. The Son is in the Father and the Father is in the Son as to relationship. The Son is with the Father and the Father is with the Son, as to fellowship. The Father is not from the Son, but the Son is from the Father, as to authority. The Holy Spirit is from the Father and the Son proceeding, as to nature, relationship, cooperation and authority. Hence, neither Person in the Godhead either exists or works separately or independently of the others."[73]

I especially like that last phrase—that no Person in the Godhead, "either exists or works separately or independently of the others." I believe this idea reinforces and undergirds the facet of the Trinity that I endeavored to highlight in this book—the Trinity's seamless, flawless teamwork that has resulted in our eternal benefit and that sets the standard for how we as believers are to work in partnership with God and with one another. I also realize that God is bigger, more awesome, and more wonderful than our best attempts to describe Him.

Jack Hayford is known for wisdom and balance in teaching Scripture, and I appreciate his rich insights:

"Scripture reveals different operations, administrations and activities of the Father, Son and Holy Spirit. Nevertheless, we cannot limit any person in the Trinity to performing certain tasks. In these various functions of the Godhead, God again surpasses the boundaries of our best understanding, refusing to be contained by the limits of human comprehension.

---

[73]http://ag.org/top/Beliefs/Statement_of_Fundamental_Truths/sft_full.cfm#2

- The Father may be seen as the Source, the Life Giver, and the Creator.

- The Son may be seen as the Substance, the Transmitter, the Communicator, the Messenger, and the Word.

- The Spirit may be seen as the Stream, the Life Breath, the Revealer, the Power and the Love of the Father.

- "Yet in all this, let us humbly remember that whatever the distinct role, action or function we perceive any member of the Godhead to exercise, the Three-in-One are always coequal, coeternal, and coexistent in being, power, and holiness."[74]

I highly value all that God has revealed to us about His nature and character, and yet I realize that "we know in part and we prophesy in part" (1 Corinthians 13:9, *NKJV*). Thank God for the part we know, but when it comes to the awesomeness and grandeur of God, we can all say with David, "Such knowledge is too wonderful for me, too great for me to understand!" (Psalm 139:6, *NLT*).

If our quest is merely to micro-analyze theological complexities, we will be perpetually frustrated and ultimately unfruitful. However, if our heart's desire is to love, worship, and serve God, we are aligning ourselves with Heaven's purpose for our lives, and we will no doubt be aided and supported with help from on High.

---

[74]Jack Hayford, Explaining the Trinity. Sovereign World, Lancaster, United Kingdom. 2012. (ebook)

PRAYER OF SALVATION

God loves you—no matter who you are, no matter what your past. God loves you so much that He gave His one and only begotten Son for you. The Bible tells us that "...whoever believes in Him shall not perish but have eternal life" (John 3:16 NIV). Jesus laid down His life and rose again so that we could spend eternity with Him in heaven and experience His absolute best on earth. If you would like to receive Jesus into your life, say the following prayer out loud and mean it from your heart.

Heavenly Father, I come to You admitting that I am a sinner. Right now, I choose to turn away from sin, and I ask You to cleanse me of all unrighteousness. I believe that Your Son, Jesus, died on the cross to take away my sins. I also believe that He rose again from the dead so that I might be forgiven of my sins and made righteous through faith in Him. I call upon the name of Jesus Christ to be the Savior and Lord of my life. Jesus, I choose to follow You and ask that You fill me with the power of the Holy Spirit. I declare that right now I am a child of God. I am free from sin and full of the righteousness of God. I am saved in Jesus' name. Amen.

If you prayed this prayer to receive Jesus Christ as your Savior for the first time, please contact us on the Web at **www.harrisonhouse.com** to receive a free book.

Or you may write to us at

Harrison House • P.O. Box 35035 • Tulsa, Oklahoma 74153

The Harrison House Vision

Proclaiming the truth and the power

Of the Gospel of Jesus Christ

With excellence;

Challenging Christians to

Live victoriously,

Grow spiritually,

Know God intimately.

Additional Teaching Resources by Tony Cooke

Available at www.tonycooke.org

Your Place on God's Dream Team: The Making of Champions - Book and Video Series

Through the Storms: Help from Heaven When All Hell Breaks Loose - Book and Video Series

Qualified: Serving God with Integrity and Finishing Your Course with Honor - Book

Grace: The DNA of God - Book and Video Series

In Search of Timothy: Discovering and Developing Greatness in Church Staff and Volunteers - Book, Video Series, Workbook

Life After Death: Rediscovering Life After the Loss of a Loved One - Book

Sign up to receive Tony Cooke's free monthly teaching articles at www.tonycooke.org